A STORY

BURN *the* PLOW

Kim Nash

TREMENDOUS LEADERSHIP
Leadership with a kick!

Tremendous Leadership
PO Box 267 • Boiling Springs,
PA 17007 (717) 701 - 8159 • (800) 233 - 2665 •
www.TremendousLeadership.com

Scriptures taken from the Holy Bible,
New International Version®, NIV®.
Copyright © 1973, 1978, 1984, 2011 by Biblica, Inc.™
Used by permission of Zondervan.

The following song lyrics were used with permission
and/or under the auspices of fair use.

"Into the Sea" © Tasha Layton. Essential Music Publishing.

"While I'm Waiting" © John Waller. Capital CMG Publishing.

"Make Room" © Meredith Andrews. Curb|Word Entertainment.

"Smile" © Sidewalk Prophets. Curb|Word Entertainment.

Kelly Johnson Photography https://www.kellyjohnsonphotog.com/

Tremendous Leadership's titles may be bulk purchased for business or promotional use or for special sales. Please contact Tremendous Leadership for more information.

Tremendous Leadership and its logo are trademarks of Tremendous Leadership. All rights reserved.

Paperback ISBN: 978-1-949033-92-2
eBooks ISBN: 978-1-949033-93-9

DESIGNED & PRINTED IN THE
UNITED STATES OF AMERICA

DEDICATION

This book is being dedicated to my dad,
David R. Logan, Sr.
(1935 – 2016)

*My dad was known for his memorable,
quick-witted responses.
One of his most famous responses was
"Are you a writing a book?"
after I would ask a question.*

*Yes, I did write a book, and I wish he could
have been here to read it.*

TABLE OF CONTENTS

1 The Prompt 1
2 The Equipping 17
3 Who Am I? 33
4 Assumption vs. Fact 49
5 Perspective 63
6 Comparison 79
7 Not This Opportunity 95
8 Relationships 111
9 Build Up One Another 127
10 Open Mind, Open Heart, Open Hands 143

Endnotes 157
Songs of Encouragement 159
About the Author 161

Chapter 1
THE PROMPT

"For I know the plans I have for you," declares the Lord,
"plans to prosper you and not to harm you,
plans to give you hope and a future."
Jeremiah 29:11

My husband and I were living a great life. We had jobs that paid well. We were empty nesters. Our four kids lived independently, and we had three beautiful grandchildren. In preparation for the next phase of our lives, we bought a piece of land, sold our house, put our things in storage, and lived in a rental townhouse while we took a year to build our new home. We were comfortable and had everything we needed and wanted, but God was about to nudge me to step out of that comfort zone.

That nudge began one weekend in October of 2013. Just like every other weekend, my husband and I went to our church. I greeted and checked children into their appropriate classes and then joined my husband in the auditorium for the praise opening of the service. Our talented worship band created a profound glorification experience where we spoke to God through song. Then we settled into our seats and listened as the pastor spoke. He announced the beginning of a new series based on the book *Greater: Dream Bigger. Start Smaller. Ignite God's Vision for Your Life* by Steven Furtick of Elevation Church. Little did I know how God would use this series to jolt me from comfort to discomfort and eventually onto a path I could have never imagined!

The Plow

Our pastor shared a passage from the Old Testament, I Kings 19:19-21, where God directed the prophet Elijah to anoint his successor. Elijah found Elisha, who was plowing his fields, and threw his cloak on him. After receiving Elijah's mantel, Elisha proceeded to kill his twelve oxen, burning his plowing equipment to cook the meat and feed the people. Then, he followed Elijah. Elisha was willing to leave behind his land, his livelihood, and his family and move toward an unknown future. At first, I wasn't sure how this applied to my life, but then I gained clarity. I realized that God's vision for me is not to be comfortable in my routine, but to step out in faith and live the life He envisioned for me. He created me for so much more beyond the comfort to which I had become accustomed.

I experienced a firm conviction that there was more I needed to surrender to His will. But what was it? What was I supposed to do? God was obviously preparing me, but I wasn't sure for what. I even questioned if I should write a book, which was crazy because writing never brought me joy. Writing papers in college was a struggle, so creating a book would certainly push me out of my comfort zone. Was that God's will for me? In all seriousness, God, what was my plow that needed burning? What was God's perfect will for my life? I began to seek the answer to this question earnestly.

The sermon series lasted several weeks, and each weekend I was excited to learn more. I thought maybe this would be the week God revealed His plan to me. Would this be the week my Elijah would show up, throw his cloak around me, and give me distinct direction as he did with Elisha? I would walk away feeling convicted each week but with no clear path to the next steps.

I knew God wanted me to be more than comfortable; He wanted me to be greater. He created me to prosper and thrive, not simply to be alive. Jeremiah 29:11 tells us that God knows His plans for us, plans to prosper and not harm us and plans to give us hope and a future. Ok, God, so why are your plans a secret? Take the suspense away, and please tell me! Make it evident as Elijah did with Elisha. But God's plans are not a secret, and Jeremiah 29:12 reveals the next step. If we stop at verse 11, we miss it. God proceeds to tell us in verse 12, "Then you will call on me and come and pray to me, and I will listen to you." The answer to my heart's desire was clear. I needed to seek Him through prayer because prayer is the bending of our will to the will of God.

I had previously experienced God's promise in this verse, so I knew it to be true. Many years before this encounter, I lived far from God's will. I was miserable and was eventually brought to my knees, crying out to God. I had to repent and turn from my wicked ways, and God was faithful and guided me to the right path beyond what I deserved. I am so glad that God's mercies are greater than my sins. God showed up in unique ways that I would never forget. I knew He would do it again, but I wanted answers now. My timing is not God's timing. God's timing is perfect, and I had to learn to wait on His answer. Ecclesiastes 3:1 tells us, "There is a time for everything, and a season for every activity under the heavens," and Ecclesiastes 3:11 confirms, "He has made everything beautiful in its time."

Isn't 'Good' Good Enough?

We finished the *Greater* book series and started a new one, but my conviction and discomfort continued. As is always the case, life got busy with other demands. I found myself focusing on building our house, going to work, and enjoying our family. I pushed burning my plow to the back of my mind. I ignored those quiet yet persistent convictions more and more and slipped back into the routine of my comfortable life. Life was good; wasn't that good enough for God? I began to rationalize that if I hadn't gotten an answer yet, perhaps I was meant to continue the way things were.

God will always find a way to get our attention, and we cannot hide from Him. We can learn from the actions of Adam and Eve. After they disobeyed God, Genesis 3:8 tells us, "Then the man and his wife heard the sound of the Lord God as he was walking in the garden in the cool of the day, and they hid from the Lord God among the trees of the garden." Playing hide and seek with God never ends well. Jonah ran from God, too. In Jonah 1:17, God sent a giant fish to swallow Jonah after he refused to preach to the Ninevites and took a defiant detour to Tarshish. Jonah found himself in the belly of the fish for three days after the sailors on his escape vessel tossed him overboard to calm the seas. Talk about getting someone's attention! God doesn't forget about us and His plans for us. He will find a way to speak to us. I am grateful that God doesn't give up and continues to show us patience and mercy.

The Prompt

As my husband and I continued with life, dynamics in my workplace were changing, and I questioned whether it was the right place for me. In reality, this discontent was God showing up yet again. He would not let me stay in my comfortable space. When I had joined my current employer several years earlier, it was a small business of 25-30 employees. The organization had an excellent reputation in the community for its customer service. I knew this firsthand because I had been a client of this organization, and I was so impressed with them that I went to work there.

It was exciting as we brought on new clients, provided more services, and hired new employees. We were having fun! Unfortunately, it did not last. When a small, independent organization in this industry is financially healthy and growing, it becomes ripe for the picking. And that is precisely what happened. A national organization acquired us. We went from being a small business with one owner to a national publicly traded company. I was not excited about the new ownership. I again sought God's counsel but still felt that it was not the time to burn my plow. Corporate left us alone to keep doing what we were doing for the first few years, but that independence did not last long.

God's Divine Pruning

During the *Greater* series at church, one of my coworkers, who occupied an essential role in the company, saw what was coming and left for another opportunity. An individual who lacked my colleague's expertise and leadership filled this vacancy. The new hire's lack of skills resulted in a decline in customer satisfaction, a loss of clients, and

Burn the Plow: A Story of Surrender

a decrease in market share. Now that we were a publicly traded company, our new shareholders were not impressed with these downward turns. In addition, our new owners entered a partnership with another company in which they received a fee for getting our existing customers to use the partner's services – a kickback in essence. Our leadership did not disclose this financial arrangement to our customers. This absence of transparency showed me that my core values no longer aligned with the organization. I found myself very uncomfortable with the crossing of ethical gray lines. I loved the clients, was passionate about my work, and appreciated many coworkers. I earned an excellent salary, had great benefits, and did not want to start a new job elsewhere. Plus, there was no guarantee another company would be any better. However, I knew I needed to explore other options, and I sent out a few resumes as time passed. Was now the time to burn the plow? And why was I not getting clarity on the next steps?

I continued to stay very tuned in for God's timing. He was teaching me patience. The previous situation where we lost one of our key personnel remedied itself as the individual returned to the company. Things seemed to be turning around for the better. The immediate situation improved, and I was hopeful that it would continue. Maybe the plow wouldn't have to be burned after all. Maybe I could gather with my core team and ride out the other areas that were incongruent with my values. But that wasn't the case. Those nudges from God were not going away, and I knew I would have to decide.

Over the next few years, God continued to show me, through a variety of negative experiences, that I was not where He wanted me. I began to ponder my next steps. It was time to evaluate where God wanted me and what He wanted me to do. The time came for me to get serious about understanding my passions, strengths, and talents. Where did God want me, and how could I use my gifts to glorify Him? I was still contemplating the book idea but thought, maybe someday! During this time, I had an opportunity to conduct training for a client traveling to locations in three states. Training and public speaking have always been my passion, and this engagement confirmed it for me.

One day on my way to work, an advertisement came on the radio promoting the John Maxwell certification program for speaking, teaching, and coaching. This caught my attention as I was familiar with John Maxwell and had read some of his leadership books. I wanted to learn more about the program, and I connected with a representative who sold me on the idea. Certification required online work followed by an in-person conference in Florida offered only twice per year. This conference would be a significant step toward my training and public speaking passion. While at the meeting, God inspired me to start my own business focusing on training/development, public speaking, and coaching to encourage others on their professional journey. The cloak passed! Now it was time for the next steps.

Almost There

When I returned home from the conference, I continued to work for my employer because I was not confident that this was the time to burn my plow. However, I did not stop thinking about the conference, and I started dipping my toe into creating my own business. Still, I was not ready for a full plunge yet. Many people identify with this tension that accompanies any life change.

The first step was to create a name for the new venture, something creative that would stand out. As my husband and I drove to North Carolina one weekend to visit our daughter and her husband, we brainstormed names. After a few hours, THriv rose to the forefront. There is really nothing significant about the spelling; I chose it because it was different and unique. As we continued to drive, I remembered that Casting Crowns produced a studio album and song "Thrive" that had really resonated with me, so this thought confirmed that my new business venture should be called THriv. That name stuck because God calls us not just to survive but also to thrive. God's vision for my life is more extraordinary, and He wants me to thrive. Therefore, this revelation has become my theme song!

For the next eight months, I continued to work full-time in the corporation, but God did not stop convicting me that I wasn't in the right place. It was time for a complete change; time to burn the plow. At the beginning of the year, God impressed upon me that I should resign from the leadership team and reduce my schedule from five days per week to four days per week with a 20% pay reduction. I presented this plan to my boss, and he agreed to it. This reduction in my full-time schedule allowed me the opportunity to spend time working on THriv. It also meant that we would see a 20% reduction in our income until I could acquire new business. In Matthew 6:25, Jesus teaches, "Therefore I tell you, do not worry about your life, what you will eat or drink; or about your body, what you will wear. Is not life more than food, and the body more than clothes?" He continues in verse 33 saying, "But seek first his kingdom and his righteousness, and all these things will be given to you as well." Again, God showed up. My husband received a promotion and a pay increase that made up almost 70% of the reduction in my salary.

Time to Go All In

This split arrangement of me working in dual roles continued for two years, and it was a challenge because I wanted to give my best to both companies. Finally, it became clear that I could not continue to serve two masters. In Matthew 6:24, Jesus tells us, "No one can serve two masters. Either you will hate the one and love the other, or you will be devoted to the one and despise the other. You cannot serve both God and money." As time went on, Jesus' words played out in my life. Through a variety of situations in my full-time position, God was showing me that it was finally time to burn the plow, leaving the security and comfort of the job I had known for 15 years, and go full time with THriv. It was the time to go all in.

I wrestled with a lot of emotions during this time. God continued to work on me as I struggled with the unknowns. He never gives up on us, and He is patient as we process His calling. I was giving up the comfort of a guaranteed paycheck every two weeks, excellent health insurance, matching 401k benefits, paid time-off, etc. If I transitioned full-time into THriv, I would have to develop the business, deliver the service, and manage the accounting. How could one person possibly handle all of this? I was so focused on financial comfort that I wasn't trusting God. That's when it hit me; financial comfort was the actual plow I needed to burn.

I will never forget the day I made a formal announcement of my plans – a burning of the plow with my existing job, if you will. It was a sunny day in May 2019. I traveled to Philadelphia to deliver training to a client. My boss and I didn't work in the same office. However, he was in our office near Philadelphia, and this trip would be the perfect time to schedule a meeting with him. I walked into his office and told him that I had decided to move full-time into THriv. I planned to leave the organization at the end of December 2019. Yes, I gave a seven-month notice for resignation. My announcement did not come as a surprise to him.

Since I was an at-will employee and did not have a contract, he could have asked me to leave at that moment, but he did not. I could have given a two-week notice, but I had a great relationship with my clients and didn't want to abandon them without putting together a transition plan to ensure they would continue receiving excellent service. When I walked out of the building that day, I felt such a weight lifted from me and had such a peace that I cannot describe. Between May and December of 2019, God continued to show up in unique ways to confirm my decision. Philippians 4:6-7 says, "Do not be anxious about anything, but in everything, by prayer and petition, with thanksgiving, present your requests to God. And the peace of God, which transcends all understanding, will guard your hearts and your minds in Christ Jesus."

As December 2019 approached, and I was ready to leave an organization I had dedicated my talents to for 15 years, I reflected on my time there. How does someone walk away from an organization where they invested so much of themselves without feeling sad or questioning their decision? Again, I referred to Ecclesiastes 3:1, "There is a time for everything, and a season for every activity under the heavens." This transition was my time, and the season was changing; I needed to move forward and trust God. I burned my plow just like Elisha did when Elijah threw his cloak upon him. I was at peace!

Learning to Listen for God

How did I know the prompting to leave my job was from God? I believe that listening to God is a very personal event, and it is different for each person. We see this revealed throughout the Bible. In Exodus 3, God caught Moses' attention by setting fire to a bush that did not burn. In 1 Kings 19, God sends Elijah. In Daniel 5, God wrote a message on the wall for King Belshazzar that Daniel interpreted for the ruler. We can't forget Jonah; God sent a giant fish to swallow him. Matthew tells us in his gospel how God sent an angel to reassure Joseph to take Mary as his wife. When Mary visits Elizabeth, Luke tells us in his gospel that Elizabeth's baby leaped in her womb and filled her with the Holy Spirit.

These are just a few examples we read about in the Bible. We may never experience a burning bush, writing on the wall, being swallowed by a big fish, or an immaculate conception. Still, I believe God shows up in ways that will get our attention! Here are things I believe allow God to speak to us:

Belief in the Holy Spirit – In the New Testament, we learn that God came to earth in the form of man to be among the people. How amazing would it be to witness Jesus performing miracles and hear him teaching in person! Although Jesus is no longer walking the earth as a human, He did not leave us empty-handed.

In Hebrews 1: 1-2, the writer tells us that in the past, God spoke to our forefathers through prophets at many times and in many ways, but in these last days, he has spoken to us through his Son. Jesus tells us in John 14:26 that the Father will send the Holy Spirit in Jesus' name to teach us and remind us of everything He has told us. We also are told in John 14:17 that if we believe, the Holy Spirit will live in us. God uses the Holy Spirit, which lives in me, to speak to me!

Openness to his voice – Although I believe God speaks to me through the Holy Spirit, I must be open and available to listen to Him. What excuses do I make not to set time aside to listen for God? Do I see God in every situation? If I am honest, I usually show up in my prayer time with a list of wants or expectations for God. But I am often reminded of what the psalmist wrote in Psalm 46:10, "Be still and know that I am God." When I am still – when I am quiet and not constantly moving, thinking, or speaking – I am able to hear His gentle voice directing me, and knowing that He is God and gives me peace.

There is a frequent reference to our "chair time" with God in my church. Chair time is a place where you can meditate, pray, journal, and be with God. I take the phrase "chair time" figuratively and not literally. I do not have a chair that I retreat to when I want to be with God. For me, chair time may be a walk through my neighborhood, on my treadmill, or the best place of all, on the beach! My "walk time" is my daily worship time listening to God. Trust

The Prompt

me – when you take the time to be still and listen to God, you will be blown away by what is revealed to you.

Scripture/Song – Not only has Jesus left the Holy Spirit in us, but we have the Scriptures. In 2 Timothy 3:16, Paul tells us that ALL Scripture is God-breathed. Paul tells us in Romans 15:4 that everything written in the past was to teach us so that through endurance and the encouragement of Scriptures, we might have hope. Reading and meditating on Scripture is mighty; I have been inspired so many times by His Word, in good times and bad. It is impossible for me to choose one favorite verse.

I am so thankful for the Christian music artists who use Scripture as the foundation for their songs. I love speaking to God through music, and a great way to remember Scripture is by having a Scripture-inspired song playing through your mind. Part of my daily worship is reading my Bible and listening to praise music. In each chapter of this book, I will share Scriptures and songs that have played an integral part in the lessons I have learned and given me direction, hope, and peace.

Prayer – In Philippians 4:6, Paul tells us not to be anxious about anything, but in everything, by prayer and petition, with thanksgiving, present our requests to God. In Psalm 34:4, the psalmist David writes that he sought the Lord, and the Lord delivered him from all his fears. Sometimes we feel intimidated before God in prayer. What if I don't say the right things, don't use the right words, or God is too busy to listen to me? These thoughts come from Satan! God wants a relationship with you. He wants you to be honest, not fake! God is never too busy for you! We can speak to

God any time, any place, and for any reason. Sometimes a friend or family member comes into my mind, and at that moment, I will stop and pray for them. Or there are times when my heart is heavy, and while I am driving, I will pray. Of course, I keep my eyes open! I even pray in the shower! God hears you wherever you are. However, God may not always answer your prayer in your timing or in the way you expect. In Isaiah 55:8, God tells us His thoughts are not our thoughts, and neither are our ways His ways.

God sees the whole picture, and we only see a small portion. Sometimes God will reveal to us that we need to change our prayer. For example, many years ago, God convicted me to change my prayer when I came upon an accident that caused a traffic delay. I was frustrated that I was going to be late for work. Instead of focusing on my inconvenience and petitioning for an on-time arrival, God revealed that being late to an appointment was insignificant in light of what the people in the accident were experiencing. They could be hurt or may have even perished. For them it could be far more serious than being late to work – they may not be going home to their family. Now whenever I come upon an accident, I stop and pray for the people involved and their families.

Counsel with Wise People – Throughout the Bible, we read about God providing counsel through people. Exodus 18 tells of the account of Jethro, Moses' father-in-law visiting him in the desert. As Jethro observed Moses, he recognized that Moses was over his head and gave him wise counsel. Moses listened to his father-in-law. King Belshazzar called on Daniel to interpret the writing on the wall (Daniel 5), and Joseph interpreted Pharaoh's dream (Genesis 41).

The Prompt

Before I started THriv, I met with a few business owners. I asked questions about how they started their businesses, what they enjoyed about being an owner, and lessons they had learned along the way. The feedback from these meetings proved very beneficial as I was starting out.

Confirmation we are on the right path – As children, we heard the story of Noah and the ark found in Genesis 6. Noah was a righteous man, blameless among the people, and walked faithfully with God. Because the people were corrupt, God planned to destroy them and the earth. God shared his plan with Noah and directed him to build an ark with specific details. Noah did as God commanded, and God spared Noah and his family.

Genesis 22 tells of yet another man who was asked by God to do something unimaginable, and he obeyed. God directed Abraham to sacrifice his son, Isaac, the Son that God had given to him and his wife Sarah late in their lives. Abraham took Isaac and prepared him as an offering, but an angel of the Lord appeared and stopped Abraham. Because of Abraham's obedience, God promised blessings upon him and his offspring. At the time of this writing, it has been three years since I burned my plow! God continues to show me confirmation of his direction.

God wants us to live a life in which we prosper, and this often requires us to move from a life of comfort and independence to a life where we trust and lean on Him. Is there something God has been convicting you to do or change and you have been ignoring His promptings? Perhaps now is the time to believe, be open, listen, read Scripture, pray, and seek wise counsel to move to the life God has planned for you.

Burn the Plow: A Story of Surrender

Reflection:
1. Do you know the plans God has for you? What is God revealing to you? (Jeremiah 29: 11-12)
2. What is the "plow" that you need to burn to follow God's direction for your life? (I Kings 19:19-21)
3. What is holding you back from fully following God? (Matthew 6:25)
4. What two masters are you serving? (Matthew 6:24)
5. What are you anxious about? (Philippians 4:6-7)
6. In what ways does God speak to you?

Songs of Encouragement:
1. "Thrive" performed by Casting Crowns
2. "Burn the Ships" performed by FOR KING + COUNTRY

Chapter 2
THE EQUIPPING

*"My grace is sufficient for you,
for my power is made perfect in weakness."*
2 Corinthians 12:9

It was evident God was prompting me to pursue a new career path. I had peace and knew that I would burn my last plow to take up a new one, but I felt unqualified as I venture into this unknow realm. This new calling was so different than anything I had experienced before. Leaving a comfortable job with a guaranteed biweekly paycheck and benefits was scary. Being an independent contractor meant I would be responsible for everything – marketing, sales, operations, accounting, taxes, IT, etc. This professional independence was truly foreign territory for me and wondered, could I do it all? I was inexperienced in each of the new areas that would fall on my shoulders in this next stage – especially the sales and marketing. This reality was most concerning because if I was not successful in sales and marketing, I wouldn't have clients. And without clients I wouldn't have a business! I was putting too much pressure on myself. I had desired to walk away from my corporate job for years. Still, I was not a salesperson, and I was uncomfortable promoting myself.

Over and over, I read Scripture talking about doubt, which was the followed by the two most beautiful words in the English language, "but God." These words signify a time when God steps in and intervenes on our behalf. Below I've shared a few verses for encouragement:

- Isaiah 41:10 *"So do not fear, for I am with you; do not be dismayed, for I am your God. I will strengthen you and help you; I will uphold you with my righteous right hand."*
- Deuteronomy 31:6 *"Be strong and courageous. Do not be afraid or terrified because of them, for the LORD your God goes with you; He will never leave you nor forsake you."*
- Psalm 55:22 *"Cast your cares on the LORD and He will sustain you; He will never let the righteous fall."*
- Hebrews 13:5b-6 *"because God has said, 'Never will I leave you; never will I forsake you.' So we say with confidence, 'The Lord is my helper; I will not be afraid. What can man do to me?'"*

A few months after leaving my corporate job, the world shut down due to COVID-19. I thought, "Really, God? Did you prompt me to leave my comfortable job and go down a path only to hit a dead end?" I watched as the world faced economic uncertainty and businesses were closed as shutdowns were imposed. Long-standing providers of goods and services were faltering, and I was supposed to start my fledgling company in the midst of such upheaval? *But God.* A global pandemic may have come as a surprise and disruption to me, but not to God. I continued to trust God repeating *I don't know, but God does.* I also did not realize that God had been equipping me for years to be qualified for this pandemic, and He would reveal His plan to me in due time.

The Equipping

Why is our first response *doubt* when God calls us? I believe this is something instilled at birth. As we progress through life on earth, we are constantly being evaluated, tested, and assessed. If we don't measure up, we are left feeling we are not good enough. For example, a newborn baby receives an Apgar score – an acronym for appearance, pulse, grimace response, activity, and respiration – within the first few minutes after they are born. Within moments of birth, that little life is already being evaluated to see if they measure up! As that baby grows, they have regular check-ups with a pediatrician to ensure they are hitting appropriate milestones in growth and development. Are they rolling over? Sitting up? Babbling? Taking steps?

Once a child is old enough to go to school, there are specific criteria they must meet to be enrolled, including motor and cognitive skills. As the child gets older, they may want to participate in sports, band, choir, theater, and other extra-curricular activities. Through try-outs and auditions, the child must demonstrate they have the skill and ability required to be part of the team or activity. As they move on to graduation, they must meet specific requirements to receive a diploma. If one wants to pursue a college degree, most schools require a minimum score on a college admissions test to qualify for enrollment. For some, the need for financial aid and scholarships may limit which college they can attend. Again, while in college, there are more requirements, classes, final exams, and internships to complete in order to earn the degree.

Finally, as adults, we are bombarded with qualifications as we enter the world. We cannot obtain a credit card, finance a car, mortgage a house, or have the utilities turned

Burn the Plow: A Story of Surrender

on until the lender checks our credit score to ensure we are qualified. To ensure that we have the financial means to pay for our homes, cars, food, and other necessities, we need a source of revenue. As we scour the job openings, many have minimum requirements to apply. When we do not get a job for which we interviewed, the message we receive is that there was someone else more qualified. We are rejected!

Conditioned throughout life by all these qualifications and rejections, it is no wonder we immediately revert to earthly standards, feel unworthy, and anticipate failure when God calls us for something outside of our comfort zone. The good news is God won't call us to do something unless He will be right there with us. He specifically calls the unqualified and equips them for success. Earthly qualifications result in rejections; Godly qualifications require obedience.

As we explore the Scriptures, we read many stories of people called by God for His purpose who, according to earthly standards, would have been unqualified and rejected. God does not call the qualified but rather the unqualified. This flipping of worldly wisdom is how He receives glory. He uses our weakness for good and demonstrates how His power qualifies us. If we achieve success any other way, we are doing it independent of Him.

The story of Moses in the book of Exodus narrates the historical account of God's deliverance of His people from slavery in Egypt. Moses' story begins with God saving him as a baby. The oppressed Israelites were growing in number so, in order to control their population, Pharaoh had ordered all male Hebrew infants be slaughtered by throwing them into the Nile River. One Hebrew mother was able to hide her baby boy for three months, but she became fearful that

The Equipping

he would be discovered and killed. So, she laid her son in a basket and placed it in the reeds along the bank of the Nile. She had Miriam, the baby's sister, keep a watchful eye over the basket.

Pharaoh's daughter went to the river to bathe and discovered the baby among the reeds. Feeling sorry for the baby when she heard him cry, she asked one of her servants to retrieve him from the water. Miriam told Pharaoh's daughter that this was a Hebrew baby and cleverly asked if she should get a Hebrew mother to nurse him. Pharaoh's daughter agreed, and Miriam returned with the boy's own mother. Once he was older, the boy was returned to Pharaoh's daughter to raise him. At this time, she named him Moses meaning "I drew him out of the water."

One day while Moses was tending the flocks, an angel appeared to him in the flames of fire in a bush. Moses was intrigued as the bush was on fire but did not burn, and he walked over to the bush. God called him by name and told him to stop and remove his sandals. Once God revealed himself, Moses hid his face because he was afraid to look at God, an act of fear rooted in reverence and respect and found throughout the Old Testament. God proceeded to tell Moses that his people were suffering, and the time had come to rescue them, and, oh, by the way, He was sending Moses to do the job!

I have tried to put myself in Moses' place and cannot imagine how I would have responded. Here I am minding my own business, and suddenly, flames come out of a bush that is not burning up. My curiosity is peaked, so I walk toward the bush then the Lord calls me by name and tells me I am being sent to rescue the Israelites from Egypt. Is this a bad

Burn the Plow: A Story of Surrender

dream? Is someone playing a joke on me? When I return home, and my spouse asks how my day was, what do I say? A typical day of tending to the flock, with one exception, the Lord appeared to me today and called me to lead His people out of Egypt – at the age of 80!

Moses did what most of us would have done. He immediately identified why he was not qualified, questioned God, and gave excuses. In fact, Moses provided five excuses.

1. Moses felt he lacked credentials (Exodus 3:11-12). As a lowly shepherd, why would Pharaoh agree to a meeting and listen to what he had to say? God knew why. He gave Moses specific instructions to first reach out to the Israelites and assemble their elders and then go with the elders to get the meeting with Pharaoh. God assured Moses that he would go before him. This would be similar to me calling the White House and requesting a meeting with the President of the United States to discuss a national policy. First, I would need to reach out to my Senator and Representative to assist me in arranging that meeting. Unfortunately, I have never had the opportunity to meet with the President of the United States, nor my congressmen. I have, however, been in situations where someone I knew introduced me to someone else and vouched for my experience and credentials. That advocacy resulted in a new client and additional business, which I believed was indeed a God encounter by placing that person into my life.
2. Moses didn't know what to say (Exodus 3:13-22) or who to say he was. God told him what to say; He provided the content. By telling the Israelites the I AM sent him and

The Equipping

the LORD the God of your fathers, the God of Abraham, the God of Isaac, and the God of Jacob has sent me to you. It is almost as if Moses had the secret code to get access. There are times when I put a proposal together, develop a training, have a difficult conversation, or write content for this book when I am not sure what to say or how to organize it. But when I focus and meditate on God, the words become clear to me.

3. Moses questioned whether the elders would believe that God appeared to him (Exodus 4:1-9). God gave him three ways to prove that God sent him: turning his rod into a snake, putting his hand into his cloak causing leprosy, and water from the Nile poured on the ground turning to blood. When I lack confidence, I remember what God has done for me in the past, and I have the confidence to trust what He will do for me in the future.

4. Moses lacked talent; he was not an eloquent speaker. He believed he was insufficient and a poor communicator (Exodus 4:10-12). At this point, God was getting a bit upset with Moses based on his response. God told Moses that He gave man the ability to speak, hear, and see. God knows better than us our strengths and weaknesses. There are times when I have been in a room where I felt inadequate, wrongly believing others were more qualified and more experienced. When asked to do something I may not have expertise in, I invest time learning how to do it and deliver the best that I can. How do we get experience if we don't have the opportunity? We need to step out and let God fill in the gaps!

5. Moses lacked commitment (Exodus 4:13). Moses asked God to please send someone else. Now God was angry,

and he told Moses to take his brother Aaron with him, who would speak Moses' words. Let's be honest – we don't like to do *hard*, and we give up too quickly instead of taking the time to invest and learn. For example, writing does not come easily to me, and to write a book? Now that was a mountain! I had no idea how the process works, but God does! I am thrilled He provided an experienced book coach to guide me on the journey. All I had to do was be obedient and follow the teacher. I am so glad God doesn't take the easy way out. He never gives up on us!

One of the key takeaways for me from Moses' story is to take my eyes off my weakness and focus on God. Where I am weak, He is strong!

In the New Testament, Jesus calls twelve unqualified men to be his disciples. These men were not elite; they were low-class, rural, and uneducated. We see God calling the humble, lowly, meek, and weak throughout the Bible. He pulled them in, equipped them, and sent them out. When Jesus left, He made sure they were not alone. He left the Holy Spirit with them. The same Holy Spirit we can have in us! These men went from their vocations to students to experts in about 18 months of training. They had no natural aptitude to be disciples and advance His kingdom. The only thing that set them apart was their willingness to follow. Even though Jesus invested in them and mentored them, it was a difficult learning process. And it will be for us as well. But that should not discourage or deter us because God will not let us fail.

None of the twelve disciples were religious teachers or scholars. They weren't preachers or missionaries or church

The Equipping

planters, as we would call them today. Yet God called them to proclaim the news of Jesus throughout the world. Here are some ways in which it seems they were unqualified, by earthly standards, for such a weighty mission:

1. **They lacked spiritual understanding.** They were slow to hear and to comprehend everything Jesus was teaching them. Jesus was patient and persistent in his instruction even knowing that Peter would deny him, Judas would betray him, and Thomas would doubt him. He never gave up on them, and the same is true for us. Jesus never gives up on us! Since Jesus is not here in the flesh today, I am not able to sit at His feet and learn like the disciples. Yet by reading the Scriptures, listening to the Holy Spirit, attending church, and participating in Bible study groups, I am able to gain spiritual understanding as if Jesus were right beside me. God's Word gives me the confidence that He will always equip me to do what He asks of me.
2. **They lacked humility.** They even argued about who would be the greatest among them. Jesus demonstrated humility by washing their feet. You and I may not be called to wash others' feet, but we are called to humble ourselves and serve others in different ways. Jesus told His disciples in Mark 9:35, "If anyone wants to be first, he must be very last, and the servant of all." Unfortunately, we live in a 'me first' world where people often lack humility and put themselves first, asking *what's in it for me.*

Instead, we should strive to live a God-first life in a me-first world. I remember hearing this challenge in a message several years ago, and it stuck with me. My comfortable corporate job was about me, not about

serving others. I needed to leave the comfortable so that I could help others.
3. **They lacked faith.** Jesus performed many miracles to strengthen the disciples' faith. We read in Matthew 14: 24-33 that after Jesus fed the five thousand, he told the disciples to take the boat and go ahead of him while he dismissed the crowd. Before meeting up with the disciples, Jesus took time to go to a solitary place to pray. When Jesus was finished praying, it was night and the disciple's boat had gone a considerable distance. To reach the disciples, Jesus walked on the water toward the boat. The disciples were frightened and thought the figure was a ghost, they did not recognize Jesus. Although Jesus called out to them, Peter wanted proof and tested Jesus to call him onto the water. Jesus called him, and Peter started toward Jesus, but was frightened by the wind. Instead of focusing on Jesus, he was distracted and began to sink. Jesus rescued him and called him out for having little faith and questioned why he doubted. For me, walking away from a guaranteed paycheck with benefits required me to walk toward Jesus and demonstrate faith! God has never failed me, even during a global pandemic when the world shut down! The opportunity for revenue continued to show up when I least expected it!
4. **They lacked commitment.** When times were tough, the disciples fled or denied Jesus. In Mark 14:66-72, we read about Peter denying Jesus three times. In Matthew 26:14-16, Judas betrayed Jesus for money. As we continue reading in Matthew 26, after Jesus was arrested, the disciples deserted him. If I were a disciple, would I have

The Equipping

denied Jesus or fled after he was arrested? Would my fear win over my commitment? I am incredibly grateful that I live in a country where I can worship Jesus without fear of persecution or death. There are places in the world today where Christ-followers are worshiping and studying in secret because they do not have religious freedom and could be put in jail or killed for their beliefs. If we are honest, we try to avoid doing hard things or experiencing hard times and often take the easy way out. I know being self-employed means there will be good times, and there will be difficulties as well. When I am experiencing a tough time, I have a choice – will I look up or will I give up?

5. **They lacked power.** Jesus knew that once He returned to heaven to be seated at the Father's right hand, the disciples would need help. Jesus left the Holy Spirit not only for the disciples but for us too! Mark 16:20 tells us that after Jesus was taken into heaven, the disciples went out and preached everywhere. The Lord worked with them and confirmed His word by the signs accompanying it. In Luke 24:49, Jesus told the disciples that He would send them what His Father had promised (Holy Spirit). As believers, we have the Holy Spirit living within us. Romans 8:11 gives us hope that the Spirit that raised Jesus from the dead is alive in us. The Holy Spirit provides us with the power to overcome our fear and be strong to do what we are called to do. There are times when I have felt inadequate as a consultant or when writing this book. I was not sure where to start or how to resolve a problem. When I took time to focus, pray, and reflect, the Holy Spirit spoke to me and gave me direction.

Burn the Plow: A Story of Surrender

Some people have strong faith and trust God implicitly. This gift makes me think of David. In Acts 13:22, we read that God chose David because he was a man after God's own heart and would do everything He wanted him to do. As a child, I remember hearing the story of David and Goliath and how an underdog was able to defeat the big, evil giant. David took a child's toy and killed the bully! We all love stories where the underdog prevails. But, as an adult exploring the story in more depth, I find there is more to learn.

In 1 Samuel 17, we read that the Philistines and Israelites were preparing for battle. They were positioned on their hills with a valley in between them. Goliath, a champion warrior from the Philistine army, emerged from camp and antagonized the Israelite military daily. Goliath was unique as he stood over nine feet tall and was equipped with all the best weaponry and armor. He intimidated and terrified the Israelites for forty days. Bullies enjoy taunting their victims, and the best way to stop the bullying is to shut the bully down. King Saul decided that the Israelites would take up Goliath's challenge. Saul provided an incentive to anyone who would go up against Goliath. The king would offer up his daughter in marriage, which came with the privilege of becoming part of the royal household.

Meanwhile, the youngest son of Jesse, David, was at home tending the sheep while his three oldest brothers served in the military. Jesse asked David, who was still a boy, to take food to his brothers, check on them, and report back on their condition. In those days, the families provided food for their relatives and others in the ranks.

As David arrived at the Israelite camp, the army prepared their positions and battle cry. After David handed off the

The Equipping

food, he ran to the battle line with the soldiers. The young shepherd witnessed Goliath bullying the soldiers and ridiculing the Lord's people. David was furious once he heard Goliath. His words were not only against the Israelite army but an assault on God.

David knew exactly what he needed to do, and he requested to go to the front line to fight Goliath. Once King Saul learned of David's request, he immediately rejected David's offer; there was nothing logical about David's request. King Saul pointed out to David that he was not qualified to fight Goliath – he was just a boy with no experience, and Goliath was a seasoned warrior. David didn't take no for an answer. He was persistent and presented his qualifications to the king. As a shepherd, David had taken on a bear and a lion by going on the offense. This behavior enraged the wild beasts, and they turned on David. But he seized them, struck them, and killed them. David equated Goliath to an animal. It was just another fight with a wild beast; therefore, he firmly believed he could deliver them from the hand of the Philistine.

After witnessing David's persistence, King Saul was impressed and gave David his blessing, allowing him to fight. Saul offered David the best battle gear, but David rejected it because he was not comfortable in it. Not only did he refuse the military equipment, but his weapon of choice was also a stick and stones – a simple slingshot. From a human perspective, David seems unprepared and sure to lose. I can only imagine the Israelite soldiers were afraid for David as he approached Goliath. I would have covered my eyes or turned my head. The encounter began with Goliath verbally attacking David and his weapon. Goliath was sure David was no match for him. However, David knew he had the advantage because God was on his side! Remember Matthew 19:26 tells us, "With man this is impossible, but with God all things are possible." David killed Goliath, which astounded the Philistine army and caused them to turn and run away.

Honestly, there have been more times in my life than I care to admit that I have placed human limitations on God and not trusted Him fully. As I grow older and have more years behind me, I have experienced God's hand in situations that encourage me to strive to have the confidence of David. I remind myself that I don't know, but God does! God called Moses, the disciples, and David and prepared them for success. We have the assurance that God will equip us for what He calls us!

Earlier I mentioned that God prepared me for the pandemic. Several years before the pandemic and before I left my corporate job, I started teaching classes online and conducting webinars and training. Once the pandemic hit, in-person courses and activities moved to online delivery. Many teachers and instructors had to transition from classroom to Zoom and were unprepared. Because of my online experience, I was already familiar with the tools and technology I needed. Although I prefer delivering in person, God provided, and I was able to have a successful year in my business.

In his book, *Unqualified*, Steven Furtick says, "God loves to work with unqualified people. Greatness is birthed from humility, not denial. Weaknesses becomes strengths when they are embraced, not ignored."

Reflection:
1. What are you being called to do?
2. What is your BUT statement?
3. Just like Moses, what excuses are you giving to God?

4. What do you need to do to invest in being qualified for what God is calling you to do?
5. In what area of your life have you been distracted like Peter and took your eyes off Jesus?
6. How can you be more confident like David?

Songs of Encouragement:
1. "Firm Foundation" performed by Cody Carnes
2. "God of the Promise" performed by Elevation Worship

Chapter 3
WHO AM I?

"God created mankind in his own image."

Genesis 1:27

When I was a child in the 1970s, my family frequented Pappy's Pizza. We loved it because it had a festive atmosphere where we got Styrofoam hats, fake mustaches, and bowties to dress like Pappy. I don't remember much about the pizza and birch beer. Still, I do fondly remember the player piano that performed ragtime tunes and the funny mirrors we stood in front of and got a good laugh at our distorted bodies. One mirror made us look very tall and skinny, while the other made us look short and stout like a square. Although Pappy's Pizza is no longer in business, you can find these mirrors at carnivals, fairs, and amusement parks. No matter how old you are, it's still fun to stand in front of these silly mirrors and view yourself in different ways.

With all the influences impacting our life on earth – cultural norms, social media, our own experiences, societal expectations, and the voices in our heads – Satan can also distort our image. But, unlike the fun-house mirrors, the distortion from these influences is very different and is not amusing. In fact, these distortions can be hurtful, resulting in a loss of confidence and causing us to stumble or stop our journey. Therefore, we need to be confident in who we are and keep those reminders in the forefront.

Burn the Plow: A Story of Surrender

Let's begin by defining who we are in our eyes. My list would look something like this, and in the order of importance to me:

- Child of God
- Christ Follower
- Wife
- Mother
- Grandmother (Gram)
- Daughter
- Friend
- Sister
- Aunt
- Cousin
- Teacher/Consultant
- Business Owner

Notice that my profession is last on the list; it doesn't define me. As a believer, my identity is in Christ. Many of these titles can change but being a child of God will not! I am comforted by Galatians 3:26-29, which states, "You are all sons of God through faith in Christ Jesus, for all of you who were baptized into Christ have clothed yourselves with Christ. There is neither Jew nor Greek, slave nor free, male nor female, for you are all one in Christ Jesus. If you belong to Christ, then you are Abraham's seed and heirs according to the promise." Galatians 4:7 also states, "You are no longer a slave, but a son; and since you are a son, God has made you also an heir." One of the many names for God is *Abba* which means Father. God is my heavenly Father. Although my earthly father is no longer with me, I know my heavenly

Father is and will never leave me. I look forward to spending eternity with Him.

God's image

In Genesis 1:27, we learn that humans are created in God's image. When I hear "in God's image," I think of a mirror and believe God looks like humans. This perspective is superficial and not of God. Our human eyes are used to judging people by their external appearance, in other words, what they outwardly reflect. According to John Kilner, author of *Dignity and Destiny: Humanity in the Image of God*, this is far from God's truth or perspective. Since the Bible does not fully define what created in the image of God entails, we tend to create our own interpretations. Rather than God having human physical characteristics, the idea "made in the image of God" reflects that people, unlike other creatures, have an emotional, spiritual, and intellectual capacity. We are created for deep connection with others by a God who desires deep connection with us.

Worldwide, we are obsessed with what we see in the mirror. As a result, we invest in skincare products, make-up, Botox, plastic surgery, haircare, weight loss products, etc. Please do not misinterpret what I'm saying; I am not judging anyone for using these products or services. In fact, I use some of these daily. The challenge is to remember that image isn't just about the outside but also about the inside. Remember, God's image is about the whole person. Galatians 5:22 states we should manifest the fruit of the Spirit: love, joy, peace, forbearance, kindness, goodness, faithfulness, gentleness, and self-control. So, the true reflection of God's image emanates from the inside out, not the outside in.

Burn the Plow: A Story of Surrender

Because we alone, above all other creations, are made in the unique image of God, He doesn't like us to have additional images! In the Old Testament, the people worshipped physical idols, statues, and other gods. This idolatry was rampant and angered God so much that the first commandment in the Ten Commandments God gave to Moses was, "You shall have no other gods before me." Maybe I don't have tangible or physical idols, but what are those things that prevent me from surrendering all to God? My desire for a secure job with a biweekly paycheck and benefits that provided a comfortable lifestyle distracted me from listening to and heeding God's call. My focus on my financial situation overshadowed my obedience to God and trusting Him to provide. My guaranteed salary became a false idol of security that became my focus.

Although I may not fully understand the concept of being created in God's image, there are places in Scripture that can provide me with guidance. I turn to the New Testament, where I can learn about Jesus because He is God in the flesh! As recorded in the Scriptures, His time on earth can provide guidance to me.

- John 1:14 "The Word became flesh and made his dwelling among us. We have seen his glory, the glory of the one and only Son, who came from the Father, full of grace and truth."
- Hebrews 1:3 "The Son is the radiance of God's glory and the exact representation of his being, sustaining all things by his powerful word."
- Colossians 1:15 "The Son is the image of the invisible God, the firstborn over all creation."

Who Am I?

- 1 John 3:2 "Dear friends, now we are children of God, and what we will be has not yet been made known. But we know that when Christ appears, we shall be like him, for we shall see him as he is."

As a Christ-follower, I use Scripture as my reference to better understand who I am in God's image.

- Galatians 2:20 "I have been crucified with Christ, and I no longer live, but Christ lives in me. The life I now live in the body, I live by faith in the Son of God, who loved me and gave himself for me."
- 1 John 3: 23 "And this is his command: to believe in the name of his Son, Jesus Christ, and to love one another as he commanded us."
- Romans 12: 9-21 provides us with the guidance of love in action, demonstrated by Jesus.
  - Love must be sincere
  - Hate evil
  - Cling to what is good
  - Be devoted to one another in love
  - Honor one another above yourselves
  - Serve the Lord
  - Be joyful in hope
  - Patient in affliction
  - Faithful in prayer
  - Share with the Lord's people who are in need
  - Practice hospitality
  - Bless those who persecute you, don't curse them
  - Rejoice with those who rejoice
  - Mourn with those who mourn

Burn the Plow: A Story of Surrender

- Live in harmony with one another
- Do not be proud
- Do not be conceited
- Do not repay evil for evil
- Live at peace with everyone
- Do not take revenge
- If my enemy is hungry, feed him
- If my enemy is thirsty, give him a drink
- Do not be overcome with evil but overcome evil with good.

Whew! That is quite a list, but this should not be viewed as a to-do list that we check off! I believe being created in God's image is to love one another, and when we genuinely love one another, this is no longer a list but the way we live life. As a sinner, I know I am not perfect, but I see these behaviors as something I can – with God's help – strive for daily.

Most of these behaviors are counter to the world, but as Christians we are told to be in the world, not of the world! In Romans 12:2, Paul tells us not to be conformed to the world but to be transformed by renewing our minds. We will see God's good, pleasing, and perfect will. It is challenging to be God-first in a me-first world (Thank you, Steven Furtick! I heard this in one of his messages, and it stuck with me).

One of my favorite questions that I ask candidates during an interview is to describe their top three essential values and why. Some are quick to answer, and others have to pause and think about it. When a candidate pauses, I often wonder if they have never thought about their values or are trying to formulate the answers they think I want to hear. Over the years, I have conducted hundreds of interviews.

Who Am I?

It is fascinating to watch people try to be something they are not or realize they have not given too much consideration to this important topic.

Why are we afraid to be authentic? I imagine that God finds it fascinating to watch me in situations where I may not be living my values. I am so glad that God's grace is more significant than all my sins!

My value strength (the ability to live out my values under challenging situations) was probably challenged the most in a secular work environment. Early in my career, I wanted to fit in and often strayed from my values by engaging in activities that were not pleasing to God. As I have progressed in my professional and faith journey, God has given me the strength to stand up for what I believe and not be afraid to live in His will. When my co-workers would go out to happy hour after work, I would not join them. I would instead go home to my husband or children. Foul language became a regular occurrence in many workplaces. Not only did I not use bad language in the workplace, but I would ask others not to use it around me. I know people thought I was a "goody-two-shoes." These may be minor examples, but I learned to speak up with confidence when situations arose that I thought were unethical or illegal. If there are situations in your organization that conflict with your values, speak up or find a place where your values align with the work environment.

A few months after I went out on my own, I started working with a human resource consulting firm as an independent contractor. I was excited to receive an e-mail from the consulting firm with my first potential opportunity to work with one of their clients. I would be assisting them

Burn the Plow: A Story of Surrender

with human resource services. I was provided limited information about the client and the assignment, but something didn't feel right. When I logged on to the client's website and learned more about their mission, I was shocked that the values directly conflicted with mine.

The services they offered were legal but outside of my convictions. There was no possible way I could accept this assignment. Let's not forget that I was beginning to build my business and earnestly looking for revenue sources. The first offer with a new business partner directly conflicted with what I stood for. Surely, this was a test from God. Was my focus God or money? When I shared this situation with my husband, he immediately said, "it's a hard no!" And I absolutely agreed!

But what was the best way to communicate to my business partner that I couldn't accept this assignment? What if they wouldn't offer me any other work because I said *no* right out of the gate? Was it wise to turn down revenue this early in the game? In the end, I stayed true to my values, trusted God, and politely declined the assignment. Today, I am happy to say that I have received other opportunities from this business partner to work with organizations more aligned with my values. God continues to provide!

This situation taught me that my character should always be stronger than my circumstances! It is essential to identify your core values before a situation arises so that you can respond appropriately and not be tempted. Know your boundaries and be prepared to stand firm on them. When we put God first, He will bless you and me just like He blessed Noah and his family for their faithfulness.

Who Am I?

In Genesis 6:9, Noah is described as a righteous man who walked with God. He was blameless among the people of his time. 2 Peter 2:5 tells us Noah was a preacher of righteousness. During this time, the earth was corrupt to the extent that Genesis 6:6 says, "the Lord was grieved that he had made man on the earth, and his heart was filled with pain." There was a hardening of the human heart, sexual perversion, murder, and other sinful behavior which angered God. God hates sin! Because of the severe corruption in the world, God decided to destroy all the people and the earth yet spare Noah and his family. This decision by God speaks to his righteousness. He does love us as much as He hates sin. Noah and his family lived in a wicked world but stayed true to their values and beliefs. God saved them from destruction because of their willingness to stay true to their convictions.

As I read the story of Noah and his family, my perception is they were living a God-first life in a me-first world. This God-centric lifestyle is as unpopular in today's world as it was in Noah's time. Noah and his family were undoubtedly considered outcasts because they chose not to participate in the corrupt activities of the time. They endured ridicule, taunts, name-calling, and other forms of persecution. Once Noah began building the ark, I can visualize people walking by it, sneering and jeering. Not only was he ostracized for not living like the world did, but he was actually building an ark. No doubt he was probably considered the laughingstock of the town! Going to the marketplace or anywhere in public was probably very uncomfortable for the family. I can picture the entire town referring to Noah's family as "those crazy people with the big boat in their yard!"

Burn the Plow: A Story of Surrender

God chose to save Noah and his family by instructing him to build an ark. First, God told Noah that all the people and the earth would be destroyed, and he needed to make an ark because he and his family would be saved. I know I would have asked God to repeat what He just said. However, since we were told earlier in Scripture that Noah walked with God, he would have been very familiar with God's voice and didn't question Him. Noah followed God's command. After all, he was already living a counter-cultural life!

God got very specific with his instructions to Noah – the wood to use, the number of rooms, the coating, the dimensions, the placement of doors, and the number of decks. All these details were to keep Noah, his wife, his sons, and their wives safe. God also instructed him to bring living creatures aboard, male and female, clean and unclean, to keep them alive. In addition, he should get every kind of food and store it. Again, Noah stayed quiet and followed God's commands. He did everything God commanded. By the way, Noah was 600 years old at that time.

God spared Noah and his family because they were good, and He wanted to restore creation to His goodness. Remember, everyone on earth aside from Noah and his family had only evil and wickedness in their minds and hearts 24/7. *The New American Commentary* by Kenneth Matthews says it best: "Noah's venture to build his vessel upon dry land while awaiting the impending floodwater demonstrates a person trusting in what cannot be seen or proven." This activity had never been done before, and there was no precedent. Biblical scholars even surmise that before the time of Noah, rain had not fallen on the earth! Now that is faith!

Who Am I?

Noah, his family, and the animals were packed and ready to go. They shut the door and then the waiting began! Day 1, day 2, day 3, day 4, day 5, day 6, and day 7, finally rain! Although God communicated that it would be 7 days until the rain started, I think Noah and his family were anxious! What were the conversations? What were the smells, the noises? All those animals are in an enclosed area. Once the rain started, they were stuck inside for forty days and forty nights, knowing that the earth and every living thing were being destroyed. What would they find after the rain stopped and the water receded? God delivered on His promise. He kept them safe. After forty days, the rains stopped. However, they had to wait until the water receded, which is believed to be another 110 days. Once the dove that Noah set out found an olive leaf, it was confirmed that the earth was beginning to come alive. When God commanded Noah, his family, and animals to leave the ark, Noah built an altar to the Lord. Noah took some clean animals and made a sacrifice to the Lord.

For the skeptic, the account of Noah and his family is a story or a fable because it seems so unlikely that such events could occur. Again, trying to view God from a human perspective never makes sense. It does seem impossible, especially living with that many animals in an enclosed vessel! Because I believe the Bible to be God's accurate, inspired word, I believe that Noah's account is true. There are numerous in-depth books on the flood event written by Biblical scholars that detail the proof of the event from a geological perspective and historical one. Plus, the New Testament repeatedly references back to Noah, so we know if it is an actual event and not an abstract allegory. For me, the takeaway from Noah is the importance of following God, living by faith, and standing for God and against sin. I am a sinner, but I am so grateful for the grace of our loving God and for sending His son to die for our sins! His grace is greater than all my sins, and I am forgiven!

Like Noah, we live in a sin-infected world where evil runs wild. The sin today isn't much different than in the days of Noah. We are experiencing sexual perversion, murder, crime, human trafficking, drugs, hatred, division, persecution, etc. Additionally, activists influence governments to normalize many of these sins by passing laws that make wickedness legal. For those of us who stand against these sins, we are persecuted and penalized if we speak out. History has shown us that corrupt civilizations do not survive. As a Christ-follower, it is difficult to stand firm in my faith as all this destruction is going on. How can I be more like Noah?

In Ephesians 6:12, Paul tells us that our struggle is not against flesh and blood, but against rulers and authorities, against the powers of this dark world, and against the spiritual forces of evil in the heavenly realms. This verse is depressing. If we stop there, it seems hopeless; we will be defeated. But there is good news if we proceed to Ephesians 6:13, we can stand our ground during the days of evil by putting on the whole armor of God!

The Armor of God

Belt of truth: We find God's truth in the Scripture. The words strengthen our core, similar to a weightlifting belt which provides stability by supporting your core. When I read, listen, or meditate on God's Word, my faith is strengthened, I am more positive, and I dare to stay true to my values. Being in the Scripture gives me hope in a dark, evil world. Satan knows Scripture. He distorts it, finds my insecurities, and gets in my head. Daily, I find myself saying, "not today, Satan!" Nothing makes the devil flee like speaking or reading the Word of God. In John 16:33, Jesus tells us that we can have peace. We will have trouble, but He has overcome the world! Thanks to Scripture, we know how the story ends, and those who are in Christ see the future as bright!

Breastplate of righteousness: The breastplate covers the soldier's torso, protecting vital organs such as the heart. Righteousness is aligning ourselves, including our hearts, to God's expectations. It is impossible to live up to God's expectations on our own. There was only one individual who did this, Jesus. Satan is constantly attacking and tempting us, and we cannot fight Satan on our own. The Bible says he is a roaring lion, seeking whom he may devour (1 Peter 5:8). We must protect our hearts. Once we confess that we need Jesus because we are sinners and believe He died to save us from our sin, we are filled with the Holy Spirit, and we have the power to stand firm! The same power that raised Jesus from the dead lives in us!

Shoes of peace: Soldiers work as a united force; they stand together shoulder to shoulder to be firm against the enemy. To be robust against our enemy, Satan, we need to be in a relationship with others to stand together. There is strength in numbers. Being surrounded by others of faith gives me peace, and we can provide each other encouragement. When we are under Satan's attacks, we need to turn to the Scriptures, pray for strength, surround ourselves with other believers, and we will experience the peace described in John 16:33.

Shield of faith: In one of my study books from Priscilla Shirer, I found a quote I wrote in the note section, "Faith is when the dots don't connect, but you do it anyway." We are stepping into a situation where we expect God to come through. This describes me exactly when I left my corporate job, steady paycheck, and benefits. As I started this new journey, it was God and me, and I knew He would come through based on my past experiences. God has never let me down, and this time would be no different. No matter what arrows, darts, or bullets are fired at me, I have faith God will protect me.

Helmet of salvation: Helmets are worn to protect a person's skull, especially the brain. When we wear a helmet, we feel confident to engage in certain activities such as riding a bike/motorcycle/scooter, climbing rocks, ziplining, playing sports, or working on construction sites or manufacturing/warehouse sites. Our salvation is future protection from eternity in the fire pits of hell. That sounds like an insurance policy, but it is much more than a fire insurance policy. 2 Corinthians 5:17 states, "If anyone is in Christ, he is a new creation, the old has gone, and the new has come." Our salvation gives us hope daily as we live life here on earth, and it protects us from the schemes of Satan.

Sword of the Spirit: God's word. The sword for a soldier is an offensive weapon, and when it is sharpened, it can pierce through almost anything. Hebrews 4:12 says, "For the word of God is living and active. Sharper than any double-edged sword, it penetrates even to dividing soul and spirit, joints and marrow; it judges the thoughts and attitudes of the heart." We can never win battles without God's word; it provides us with the right direction. When Jesus was in the desert after fasting for forty days and forty nights, he was hungry, and Satan tempted him. Jesus rebuked him with God's word and was victorious.

Sometimes the world's evil can be overwhelming, and we lose hope. Standing on our values when others around us are giving in to sin and corruption, and even making sin legal, can cause us to fall. We need to remember who we are, stand for our values, and put on the armor of God daily.

Reflection:
1. What does your 'who I am' list reveal?
2. What characteristics/values are important to you? What would you identify as your core values?
3. What change are you afraid to make and why?
4. Can you remember a time when you begrudgingly made a change but then realized it was one of the best things you have done?
5. What "idols, statues, or gods" are you worshipping that distracts you from God?
6. Do your financial transactions and your social media posts depict who you are?
7. What can you do daily to stand firm in your values and beliefs and not be tempted?

Songs of encouragement:
1. "Who You Say I Am" performed by Hillsong Worship
2. "Image of God" performed by We Are Messengers
3. "Build a Boat" performed by Colton Dixon

Chapter 4
ASSUMPTION VS. FACT

"But blessed is the one who trusts in the Lord, whose confidence is in him."

Jeremiah 17:7

Entering seventh grade was a huge change for me. Seventh grade meant students moved from elementary school to junior high. No longer was I in a small school with neighborhood friends, as there were multiple elementary schools feeding into one junior high. Instead of being in a single classroom all day, we moved to a new room for each class. We had to learn the locker combinations, meet new teachers, learn our way around a maze of hallways, follow the new rules, and form new peer groups. Students were divided into sections, and each section attended classes together throughout the day. If I remember correctly, there was no one in my section from my elementary school; I knew no one. I won't lie. It was a hard adjustment for me. I wasn't fond of change, and I liked familiarity. I was uncomfortable. What if no one wanted to be my friend? What if the other students made fun of me? What if I didn't fit in? What if I couldn't get my locker to open and I was late for class? Needless to say, I had a lot of anxiety.

During this time of uncertainty and upheaval, something happened that changed my life. I became friends with a girl named Beth, and she invited me to church with her family. This was not the first time I went to church; my mom always took me to church from the time I was a baby. I went to church and Sunday School mostly every Sunday. In the summer, I attended "Vacation Bible School," hopping from one church to another. I sang in the children's choir, went through confirmation, and joined the church. But Beth's church was different. I would go home with Beth Wednesdays after school, and we would all pile in the family car and head to church for dinner and youth group. The first difference for me was going to church on a Wednesday night and with the whole family! My mom and I went to church on Sundays, but my dad never went with us, even on Christmas and Easter.

It felt great to go to a church with a family. Everyone in the family was involved in the church. Beth's family was awesome from my perspective; why couldn't I have a family like Beth's? I continued to attend church with Beth's family on Wednesdays and participate in youth group activities. In August 1981, a few of us from the church youth group went to youth camp in Findley, Ohio. It was at this event that I accepted Jesus and became a believer. I don't remember a lot about that evening. We were in a gymnasium because I remember sitting on the bleachers and walking from the bleacher to the stage to profess that I accepted Jesus. But I remember the most important aspect – that life-changing decision to let Jesus be Lord of my life!

That fall, when we started high school, Beth and I went to separate high schools and went our own ways. I continued to go to church with my mom. However, the church was not like Beth's, and my faith was not growing. Fortunately, there were other opportunities to go to what I call Bible-believing and-teaching churches while in high school.

Assumption vs. Fact

Once I got married, my husband and I joined a church that was Bible-believing and-teaching, and my faith grew. Even though I was baptized as an infant, I chose to be baptized again as an adult to publicly profess my faith. I have always been thankful for Beth and her family inviting me to their church and introducing me to Jesus in a different way – through the Scriptures!

No family is perfect. Families are made up of imperfect people, and we all sin. I knew Beth's parents divorced, but I didn't know the details. Many decades later, I would learn what I had believed about Beth and her family was based on erroneous assumptions. My heart broke for Beth as she shared her story on Facebook. All that time I had been attending church with Beth, she was not a believer. I had never asked her about her faith. I assumed because she went to a Bible-believing church, she was a Jesus follower. There was a lot of hurt and anger that Beth carried around that I never knew about. I was shocked and saddened! She had been in horrible situations before I met her as a young girl, and she found unhealthy ways to cope with the pain and hurt.

She hid it well from me and others. As she continued through her young adult life, she engaged in behavior that was not God's desire for His children. Not only was she hurting herself, but others as well. By this point, she was a single mom with a young daughter. She struggled financially, emotionally, and spiritually; she was helpless and drowning! Finally, one night as a last resort, she had nowhere else to turn, and she cried out to God. As I read her story, I was reminded of the story of the prodigal son told in Luke 15 and imagined the joy of a parent whose lost child has finally returned home. In Luke 15:22, when the father saw his son in the distance, he ran toward him, threw his arms around him, kissed him, a had a huge celebration. God was elated when Beth chose to stop doing her life her way and trust Him. Heaven celebrated for Beth that day!

I share this story for two reasons. First, what we see on the surface is not always true. Second, we assume that God can't use us because we are imperfect or aren't following Him fully. This is a lie from Satan. He constantly fills our heads with lies about God not being able to use us because of what we have done in the past or because we aren't good enough. As a result, we carry feelings of shame, guilt, and unworthiness. When we give in to Satan's lies, we miss out! If I believed Satan's lies, I would not have taken my leap of confidence.

Many years ago, when I moved into a human resource consultant role, there were many times I lacked confidence. Why would someone seek my advice? What made me qualified? Did I have enough experience? What if I gave the wrong direction? Should I fake it until I make it? What if I failed? I found myself making many assumptions about other people and what they might think instead of being true to who I am and trusting God. As I have grown in my profession and faith, I can focus on God and who I am. Although assumptions continue to creep into my head, I can recognize and evaluate them. Below are three erroneous assumptions that affect me and maybe you too.

1. God can't use someone like me

One of my struggles is understanding the amount of grace God pours out on us. I know I struggle because I try to put a

Assumption vs. Fact

human perspective on God and question how He can forgive me for things I have done in my past. Because of those sins, I feel unworthy to serve God. Although humans may find it hard to get past certain sins, God always welcomes us back when we turn away from the sin and run toward Him, as with Beth and the prodigal son.

The account of Paul's conversion from Saul is an amazing story of God's grace. Saul was a murderer who persecuted and killed Christians. He was out to destroy the church. Acts 8:3 tells us that Saul began to destroy the church and went from house to house, dragging men and women from their homes and into prison. Then, in Acts 9, something miraculous occurred as Saul traveled to Damascus, where he was looking for Jesus' followers to arrest.

The Lord stopped Saul in his tracks with a bright light. I imagine brighter than a strong lightning bolt. It was so bright he fell to the ground! A voice called out to him, and I find it fascinating that Saul knew who it was! The Lord caused Saul to be blind and directed him to the city for further instructions.

If I put myself in Saul's place at that moment, I imagine I would have been terrified to go to the city as God instructed. After everything Saul did to Jesus' followers, what lay ahead of him? But, again, this is a human perspective, not a God perspective. As humans, we focus on punishment. God is loving and forgiving. There are consequences, but God's grace pours over us. Romans 5:20 says, "But where sin increased, grace increased all the more." No, this does not mean it is acceptable to sin more. That would be an abuse of God's grace. Instead, this verse confirms that God's grace is greater than all my sins!

Burn the Plow: A Story of Surrender

We are told that men were traveling with Saul, and they led him to the city since he was blind. The Lord called to Ananias to accompany Saul. Ananias was aware of who Saul was and his mission, so Ananias questioned the Lord, and rightfully so. Anyone of us would have done the same! Because of Saul's reputation, Ananias assumed Saul would arrest him and put him in prison or kill him. Instead, the Lord assured Ananias that Saul had been chosen. Ananias did as the Lord commanded and met with Saul.

When Ananias placed his hands on Saul, the scales fell from Saul's eyes, and he was baptized and began his spiritual journey to lead people to Christ. It wasn't an easy journey for Saul, now Paul, to switch sides. The Jews tried to kill him, and the disciples did not trust him based on their assumptions of him. Paul traveled thousands of miles and was imprisoned, beaten, and threatened. Still, he continued to stand firm and defend and preach the gospel.

This is a fantastic story of a man transformed from someone who hated and persecuted Christians into someone who boldly and valiantly shared the good news of Jesus with the Gentiles, even at the risk of persecution and death! Paul wrote half of the books in the New Testament. God did not abandon Paul because of his past deeds but instead used him in unbelievable ways to spread the gospel, both in the early days of the church and today through the Scriptures.

The truth is no matter what I have done in the past, God forgives and pours His grace on me, and with help from the Holy Spirit, I can go on to serve Him in ways that I will never imagine. God uses my brokenness for good! In 2 Corinthians 12:9 we read, "For my power is made perfect in weakness." It took me many years to accept this truth and

Assumption vs. Fact

push Satan's lies out of my head. Satan continues to creep back in, but I recognize when it is happening, and I can shut those lies down before they get too embedded.

2. I am going to fail

For many years, co-workers, clients, and friends would encourage me to step away from my employer and start my own business, going out on my own. What was stopping me? As I reflected, it was clearly the fear of failure! I began to contemplate what I was so afraid of. For me, it was two things. First, if I failed, I would not have income. How would I pay my bills? I am not someone who is out to make as much money as possible. My financial goals are relatively simple – give 10% back to God, remain debt-free, pay my bills on time, save for retirement, and take a few vacations per year. But what if my business venture could not support those objectives? Second, I believed failure would be a personal reflection of me. It would be embarrassing, especially if my failure was public. I would lose my credibility. What would people think about me? For me, failure meant embarrassment and shame. Once I recognized I was being held back by fear of failure, God changed how I thought about it.

This mind shift occurred following a photo session with my friend Kelly, a professional photographer, who was taking photos for me to use in my business. One of the locations for the photo session that I was especially drawn to was the local train station. Kelly asked about my interest in the train station and my objective. I explained that these photos were about my personal and professional journey, and the train represented the journey. The train station was only one stop in our photo session, but one of the photos from the train station caused me to look at failure differently.

The train station had been recently restored and had some beautiful doors. I had the idea to have Kelly take a photo of me holding one of those doors open. At the time of the image, I thought it was just a fun pose. But, over the next few days, as I reflected on the photo session and viewed the pictures, the photo of me opening the door made me think of opportunities. We have to walk through doors in order to move forward on our journey, but we are held back due to fear. As a result, we miss so many possibilities. We are hesitant to walk through those doors because we don't know what is on the other side. As I thought more about fear, God revealed to me thoughts that emotion stirs up inside of me.

Failure – What have we been taught about failure? It represents embarrassment and shame, something we should hide from others. In some organizations, failure could result in a loss of a job. But perhaps failure should be viewed as a stepping stone to success. Failing is an opportunity to learn. For example, Thomas Edison failed 10,000 times while inventing the incandescent electric light bulb. He didn't view each attempt as a failure, but instead, he found 10,000 ways it didn't work! I definitely would not have had the patience to try that many times, but I am glad Mr. Edison had more tenacity than me! A more public example is Milton Hershey. He had two failed businesses before the founding of The Hershey Company. Viewing failure as a source of embarrassment and shame will likely prevent me from trying again. Whereas, if I view failure as an opportunity to learn what works and what doesn't and how to do it better, I will be more inclined to give it another shot.

Assumption vs. Fact

Emotion – Oh, the negative voices or thoughts in our head! Those thoughts tell me others are more qualified than me or that no one is interested in what I have to say or write. They tell me I will embarrass myself, I should stay within my comfort zone, and that I am not good enough. These voices and thoughts can be compelling and crippling! When these negative voices or ideas swirl inside your mind, recognize them and call them out. I have learned to be aware of these thoughts as they start to creep in, and I stop and say, "no, not today." Reading and learning Scripture or listening to uplifting music is a powerful way to replace those negative thoughts with positive and encouraging ones. There are so many Scriptures that speak to me, but I will share a few of my favorites:

> **Philippians 4:13** "I can do all everything through him who gives me strength."
>
> **2 Timothy 1:17** "For the Spirit of God gave us does not make us timid but gives us power, love, and self-discipline."
>
> **Proverbs 3:5-6** "Trust in the Lord with all your heart and lean not on your own understanding; in all your ways submit to him, and he will make your paths straight."
>
> **Jeremiah 29:11** "For I know the plans I have for you," declares the Lord, "plans to prosper you and not harm you, plans to give you hope and a future."

When those negative voices and thoughts appear, replace them with your favorite Scripture or positive thoughts.

Anxiety - If we continue to allow the negative voices and thoughts to take control, we may experience anxiety, which

Burn the Plow: A Story of Surrender

is a persistent worry and fear about situations. Symptoms may include fast heart rate, rapid breathing, sweating, and trembling to mention a few. For many people, public speaking can cause anxiety. I am the exact opposite. I love public speaking; it actually energizes me! For many years, I had difficulty empathizing with people who feared public speaking until I experienced anxiety over the fear of heights. All my life, I have had a fear of heights. I never climbed trees, playground equipment, or ladders as a child. A few years ago, my husband and I were in Pittsburgh, Pennsylvania, and he took me to a place that overlooked the city. It was a gorgeous view. However, once we parked the car and began walking toward the lookout, I felt my heart begin to race, my breathing was challenged, and I was finding it hard to move forward. My brain was sending a warning sign to my body to stop; there was danger ahead. At that moment, I realized I was experiencing anxiety, and I understood that this must be what people with fear of public speaking go through too.

I have always wanted to zip line, but the fear of heights stopped me. We recently had an opportunity to go on a cruise in which the ship had a zip line. I decided to overcome my fear and push through my anxiety and zip line. The day came, and I got harnessed up and ready to take that step. Anxiety caused me to freeze. I looked at the employee helping me and told her I couldn't do it. She was very encouraging, and I took the step! I had never been so scared in my life. When I got to the other side, the landing was not very graceful. My legs were like rubber, and I couldn't stand, but I did it! I went back later in the day and did it again. Learning to overcome our anxiety can open doors to new experiences and opportunities we don't want to miss!

Assumption vs. Fact

Robs us of opportunities – When we let our fear of failure, negative thoughts, and anxiety take over, we miss out on opportunities. Not only do we miss out on the scenic views, fun activities, and learning opportunities, but we miss out on the blessing God has for us. Some of those opportunities or benefits we will never know about. We can't spend our time living in the past and regret those missed opportunities, but we can learn from them. So, when we hear/feel God's prompting, we should respond.

From the time God first prompted me to write this book to when I finally got serious about writing it, many years had passed. During that time, many assumptions had formed in my head. I had never considered writing a book before God's prompts and had no experience. I wasn't sure where to start, who would read it, or why anyone would be interested in what an inexperienced writer had to say. Did I have enough valuable content to share with a reader? What would be the book's objective? Maybe my procrastination was a result of my assumptions. Then, right after my photo session, I had an opportunity to attend a luncheon event. The speaker challenged us to set goals and put action steps in place to make them happen. This speech inspired me, and I immediately wrote down four goals for the new year with action plans to make them happen.

Those four goals were posted in my office so I could see them every day. One of those goals was to write the book that I had been putting off for years. So, what did I need to do to make it happen? First, tell people I was writing a book so they could hold me accountable, and second, find a book coach who could give me guidance and direction (and, again, hold me accountable). As I focused on these two action steps, God surrounded me with Godly people who supported me, including an amazing book coach who has been such a blessing to me!

3. My perception is reality

As an HR professional, I have had the opportunity to interview hundreds of people over the years. The hiring manager and I would assess whether a candidate would be successful in the position, sometimes after just one interview. Although I haven't tracked my success rate in hiring, I know there were many great hires, and then there were times when it was a wrong decision for the employer and the employee. When a poor decision is made, it is important to review where we can improve the process. One practice I incorporate in the hiring process is to make sure at least two people have the opportunity to meet and talk with the candidate. Including more than one person in the interview process helps to ensure individual biases and assumptions are challenged, especially first impressions.

Let's be honest. We make judgments based on first impressions without hearing the person's story! As the saying goes, "we don't have a second chance to make a first impression." I believe God sees this entirely differently!

- John 7:24: Jesus was being criticized for performing a miracle on the Sabbath and responded, "Stop judging by mere appearances, and make a right judgment." This is a clear directive that I need to listen to the person and understand their heart, not just evaluate them by their physical appearance or the one brief interaction I had with

Assumption vs. Fact

them. For example, one time, I was in a line of people waiting to use the restroom. I asked the woman in front of me a question, and she ignored me. My first impression of her was she was rude, but I was wrong. She was deaf and didn't hear me. How often do we see people dressed in old, dirty, torn clothes or they have tattoos and piercings everywhere on their bodies? What is our first impression, or how are they stereotyped? Remember, Jesus told us to stop judging by appearance!
- Matthew 7:1-3: "Do not judge, or you too will be judged. For in the same way you judge others, you will be judged, and with the same measure you use, it will be measured to you. Why do you look at the speck of sawdust in your brother's eye and pay no attention to the plank in your own eye?" In Patrick Lencioni's *book, Five Dysfunctions of a Team*, he describes fundamental attribution error as the tendency of human beings to attribute the negative or frustrating behaviors of others to their intentions and personalities while attributing our own negative or frustrating behaviors to environmental factors. In simple terms, we believe others have control of their behaviors and choose to act the way they do. Still, when it comes to our own bad behaviors, we make excuses – I was tired/hungry/upset/hurt – or we blame others for our actions.

The three erroneous assumptions I have shared are not an all-inclusive list. There are many more situations in which I find myself making assumptions. I am sure this is true for you. We all make assumptions about situations based on our experiences or our view of the case, but our perspective is not always reality. We do not always know the entire story or see the entire picture. Satan thrives on getting into our heads and promoting negative self-talk or tricking us into judging others. We need to pause and reflect when this happens, call it out, and change the narrative. In most cases, if not all cases, we do not have the whole story when we are judging others. Perhaps, we should take the time to listen and see the situation from their perspective.

Reflection:
1. In what areas do you need to seek forgiveness to be free?
2. What are the lies that Satan tells you that hold you back?
3. What have you been taught about failure?
4. What is God prompting you to do, but you are hesitant to move forward?
5. What is an opportunity or blessing you missed out on because of fear or anxiety?
6. Where are you judging others before learning about their situation?
7. Describe a time when you made an assumption about something or someone and discovered you were completely wrong.

Songs of Encouragement:
1. "Evidence" performed by Josh Baldwin
2. "Fear is a Liar" performed by Zach Williams

Chapter 5
PERSPECTIVE

"Praise the Lord. Give thanks to the Lord, for he is good; his love endures forever."
Psalm 106:1

Do you have a happy place, a place where you can go to relax, be quiet, and gain perspective? My happy place is walking on an empty beach with the waves crashing, the sand squishing between my toes, the warm sun on my face, and the fresh smell of the ocean. Walking along the beach, I feel closest to God. We share a fantastic time of worship, talking and listening through song and Scripture. Being alone with God while enjoying His beautiful creation often changes my perspective.

I have one particularly vivid memory of such a time. My husband and I were vacationing in Myrtle Beach, South Carolina in late spring, before the summer rush, when God revealed something I needed to learn. Walking on the empty beach, I noticed an abundance of seashells concentrated in a particular area. It was almost as if a huge wave had crashed onto the beach and dumped those seashells all in one place. Seeing seashells on the beach is common, but God prompted me to stop and look closely at all these shells. I noticed the majority were crushed, having succumbed to the turbulence of the rough water. As I continued to study them, I noticed there was an occasional intact shell among the broken ones.

How did those few shells remain whole while all the ones around them were crushed into smaller pieces?

Those broken, imperfect shells spoke to me because I tend to be a perfectionist. My approach has been if you can't do it perfectly, don't do it at all. However, I have learned over the years that if we wait for perfection, we will never move forward, and we will miss opportunities to serve God and others. Now, I am learning to focus on progress over perfection! As I studied those crushed shells with an occasional whole shell in the midst, I realized that perfection is rare, but there is still beauty in the imperfect.

Progress won't happen unless we start somewhere. Taking a leap to start my own business away from my corporate position would not be perfect, but it would be progress – one step at a time. Yes, there would be turbulent waters to navigate and I could end up getting crushed but ultimately, I could trust God to carry me through those waters unbroken. By keeping my focus on God, I could survive the turbulent waters!

In Mark 4:35-41, Jesus and his disciples left the crowds to go to the other side of the lake. Jesus went to sleep, obviously exhausted from his day of ministering. Then, a furious storm came up, causing the waves to break over the boat. The disciples were afraid and woke Jesus. How could Jesus sleep through all of this? The disciples' perspective was that He didn't care if they drowned. When they woke Him, He calmed the winds and waves. Jesus then asked them why they were so afraid. Did they not have faith? Again, I am reminded that no matter how tough it gets, God is right there with me, and I can trust He will get me where I need to be. It may not be where *I* want to be, but it is where *He* wants me to be.

Perspective

Have you ever been in a season where you wondered why something is happening? Do you ask why or what God wants you to learn there? Yes, and yes! These are the times I focus on the promise found in Jeremiah 29:11, "For I know the plans I have for you, plans to prosper you and not harm you, plans to give you hope and a future." As I meditate on this verse, it turns the "Why is this happening to me" to "God, what do I need to learn here?"

One man in particular questioned God, and for good reason. Job was a man described as blameless and upright. He was a strong leader in his family and community. Additionally, he was wealthy. He had seven children, seven thousand sheep, three thousand camels, five hundred yoke of oxen, five hundred donkeys, and many servants. He was well known and respected in the region. But in an instant, it was all gone! He lost everything. If that wasn't enough, his body broke out with painful sores. It is easy to speculate what we would do if this happened to us, but until we are in the situation, we don't know.

So, what did Job do? He praised the Lord! In Job 1:21, Job took off his robe and said, "Naked I came from my mother's womb, and naked I will depart. The Lord gave, and the Lord has taken away; may the name of the Lord be praised." In the *Maxwell Leadership Bible*, John Maxwell explains Job's response by describing him as a disciplined person. Maxwell writes, "He lived his life from his character, not his emotions. He maintained perspective when tragedy struck him." What does that mean? Job was in excruciating pain, and he was suffering just as we would! His wife questioned him about maintaining his integrity. She wanted him to turn against God. In Job 2:10, Job told her that she was foolish, saying, "Shall we accept good from God, and not trouble?" Through all his trouble, he never sinned against God! His friends came and sat with him to comfort him, and no one said anything. Job didn't speak for seven days and nights because he was suffering. When Job spoke, he cursed the day he was born and wished he were dead. We can all empathize with Job; his losses were unbearable!

Job's friends may have meant well by coming to comfort him in his time of despair. However, instead of encouragement, they questioned him. They believed Job must have done something to deserve such suffering and that God was punishing him. Outwardly, Job was righteous; therefore, there must be hidden sin somewhere. His misguided friends were leading him down the wrong path. Yet Job focused on God by remembering all that He had done for him. Job's example is one of living his life based on his character rather than reacting to his circumstances. Job was full of emotions, yet he didn't allow them to control his response to his suffering. He didn't allow the change in his circumstances to change his view of God. I love that he sat quietly for seven days. He didn't complain to everyone he saw. He didn't go along with the thoughts of his wife and friends, and he didn't fly into a rage condemning God!

God does not promise us a life free of pain and anguish this side of heaven! In fact, quite the opposite. In John 16:33, Jesus tells us that we will have trouble in the world. But He also reassures us that He has overcome it. We will experience suffering but not alone; He will be with us. When those turbulent times come, I try to reflect on good times as Job did. I'm not always successful. Sometimes I lack

Perspective

confidence as I take on a project or when the outcome isn't what I expected or someone makes a negative comment about me that is hurtful. After a time of self-pity, I work to shift my focus from the bad to the good, remembering how God has provided repeatedly. During those times of self-pity or frustration, I realize that I have not focused on God but instead on the circumstance. It is time for a perspective change. Rather than ruminate on what was going wrong, I need to meditate on Paul's words in Philippians 4:13, "I can do all things through Christ who strengthens me."

Not only am I a perfectionist, but I also tend to be a people pleaser. My desire is for everyone to see me positively. As a coach, trainer, speaker, and teacher, I spend significant time preparing so those I interact with are pleased with my work. In these positions, I receive constant feedback. This input can be difficult when the feedback isn't positive, but constructive feedback is essential for growth. The purpose of constructive feedback is to provide honest and helpful ways in which someone could improve. It is a learning opportunity. Unfortunately, not everyone provides constructive feedback in such a way that it feels helpful. Some criticism can feel personal and hurtful. As someone who tends to be a perfectionist and people pleaser, I could receive ten remarks, of which nine were positive and one was negative. Where do I spend my time? On the one negative comment! Perspective is critical because if I let criticism cripple me, I will stop and not move forward and grow. I am learning to focus on the positive comments to strengthen those areas, and I try to learn from the negative ones.

Burn the Plow: A Story of Surrender

Through Job's losses and pain, he maintained perspective, but how? John Maxwell provides a model that can help us:

1. **Worship** – Job worshipped God and articulated God's sovereignty in his life. Worship doesn't always occur in a church building. Worship is spending time with God expressing your love for Him through Scripture, music, prayer, and quiet time. I love worshipping God in my church, but that is only once per week. I can worship God every day in any place, even in my car!
2. **Perspective** – Perspective allowed Job to see his limited knowledge. As a human, I am guilty of putting human limitations on God. Just like Job, I can only see the present and the past. I don't know the future, but God does. I need to remember that He has been there for me before and He will see me through again.
3. **Humility** – Humility caused Job to hunger and seek God's insight. When I am in turbulent waters, do I try to navigate myself, or am I willing to call out to God? During these times, transitioning from my self-pity means not focusing on my circumstances but rather on what God is teaching me.
4. **Teachability** – Teachability ultimately led Job to gain victory over his losses. In Job 42, he admitted to God that He spoke of things Job did not understand. But because he listened to God, questioned God, and God answered, Job could understand God's ways. When we humble ourselves, are open with God, and listen to Him, He will show us what we need to learn. It may not be the lesson we want, but it is the lesson we need!
5. **Victory** – Spoiler alert! In the end, God blessed Job by providing him with twice as much as he had before. Job

Perspective

had to be broken to acknowledge his wisdom. knowledge was limited. But when he humbled his broken self before God, Satan was defeated and God was glorified!

God was angry with Job's friends for misrepresenting Him to Job and made them atone for their folly through sacrificing burnt offerings. Although his friends questioned him and tried to distort Job's perspective of God, Job stayed strong and focused on God. Not only did Job avoid being led down a wrong path by his friends, but he also prayed for them! Because Job remained faithful to God and concerned for his friends, God restored his fortunes, twice as much as he had before.

We will experience difficult times and loss in this life, but hopefully not to the extent of Job. During times of turbulence, we need to focus on God; He is faithful. In Psalms 9:10, David writes, "Those who know your name will trust in you, for you, Lord have never forsaken those who seek you." We have the advantage of reading Job's story after God blessed him. But how do I stay focused on God and His perspective during challenging times before I know how the situation will end?

I was excited to launch my full-time business on January 1, 2020. I had a plan that would allow me to conduct training all over the country. I would be able to combine two of my favorite activities as a vocation: travel and training! This was God's plan for me, I was sure. Unfortunately, it quickly came to a screeching halt when the world shut down on Friday, March 13, 2020. Little did we know at the time what was ahead of us. When the first shutdown occurred – the two-week shutdown – I was skeptical. But I knew we wanted to make sure the medical professionals could prepare, and most of all, we wanted to save lives. When the initial shutdowns continued to be extended, I was not OK being stuck in my home office that once used to be a bedroom! I started questioning why God would prompt me to walk away from a comfortable job to pursue my passion only to shut the world down so I could not.

Soon, 2020 became the year of networking for me. It is difficult to work and network while stuck in your home. How do you stay focused on the goodness of God in times of struggle? I am an extrovert and love being with people. Isolation from others is not easy for me. When the self-pity was creeping in, I would look for opportunities to hear from God. It was amazing how God would bring people, songs, Scriptures, or thoughts that would encourage me when I needed them. Here are the top three of the many ways God showed up.

First, technology provided opportunities for me to continue to connect with others, although it was not the same as being in person! I appreciated our church's investment in enhancing the online presence so we could experience worship. During the summer, our church began hosting outdoor worship nights where we could be together in person (while maintaining physical distancing!) and it was amazing to be with other believers in that setting. In the fall, we re-opened the children's ministry and welcomed them back to the building. For those of us who served in the youth ministry, there was a sneak preview one night of what it would look like with the COVID protocols when the kids returned. That was the first time I had walked into the

Perspective

building in months; I cried. It wasn't about the building, but rather a step forward of being with people again in a familiar environment worshipping God!

Second, I was grateful that God provided opportunities for me to continue delivering training for my clients during this time. I would spend countless hours a day conducting virtual training sessions. This scenario was not my preferred method of interacting with clients, but it was where God wanted me at that time. During a time of self-pity, I listened to a podcast where the speaker asked, "When we are in the waiting phase, what are we doing to prepare for the next one?" Yes, this is the perspective that I needed. God didn't derail my plans; this was an opportunity to use the shutdown to prepare myself for the next phase. This perspective encouraged me to find creative ways to network with people in person, which improved my outlook immensely! I could balance my virtual sessions with in-person networking.

Third, I continued listening to praise and worship music. We are so blessed to have positive worship music today! When I am in my office and not in a virtual meeting, I play contemporary Christian music. One afternoon when I was having one of those self-pity moments, I heard a new song that caught my attention. The lyrics of "Into the Sea" sung by Tasha Layton were precisely what I needed at that moment; I needed hope that everything would be OK.

Though the mountains may be moved into the sea
Though the ground beneath might crumble and give way
I can hear my Father singing over me
It's gonna be OK, it's gonna be OK

Burn the Plow: A Story of Surrender

This was one of the many songs that encouraged me then and still does today. I am so grateful for all the Christian artists who have the gift to write and perform music that nurtures us.

I recognize that as you are reading my COVID experiences, they are minor compared to what others experienced during the pandemic. COVID was devastating. Lives were lost, families were forever changed, businesses failed, friendships were strained, and the toll on our collective mental health was incalculable. For many, life post-pandemic will never be the same. Although many members of my family contracted COVID, there was no loss of life, for which I am very grateful! I know there are some questioning why God would allow so much loss. I do not have the answer, but I do know that God sees the bigger picture far beyond what I know.

As positive as I tried to stay, however, my hope dwindled as COVID lingered. Like so many of you, I wondered would we ever get back to our pre-COVID lives? The answer is no! I had to accept that life as we knew it would not go back to pre-COVID. Once I began to internalize that life would not be the same, I recognized I needed to find a new path. The plan I had in January 2020 would no longer work in the post-COVID world.

The truth is that any time we go through a significant event, it changes us forever. The morning of September 11, 2001, changed each of us as we watched airplanes strike both towers of the World Trade Center and the Pentagon, as well as the flight that crashed in a field in Shanksville, PA. The United States had not experienced an attack of this magnitude on our soil since Pearl Harbor in 1941. In those horrific moments, the lives of the family members of the

Perspective

people who died in the terrorist attacks changed forever. Air travel immediately stopped, and planes were grounded for several days. We were glued to our televisions, watching the rescue and emergency teams searching through the rubble for anyone still alive and working to recover bodies. Those are images we will never forget. Would we feel safe again? When air travel reopened, the added security measures served as a reminder that we weren't as safe as we once believed. Again, why would God allow so much devastation, destruction, and loss?

If we focus on God during these times of difficulty, we can see God's goodness. I remember how the country rallied together – the groundswell of unity, compassion, and patriotism that surged in the days and weeks that followed. People were standing in long lines to donate blood, turning to God, attending church, and caring for their neighbors and family.

As devastating as COVID was in so many ways, some positive changes occurred in its wake too. For example, many people re-evaluated their priorities and realized they were spending too much time working and not enough time with their families. People wanted more flexibility with their work schedule, and if their employer could not provide a greater balance, they would find opportunities elsewhere. Many people left the workforce by retiring or starting their own businesses. Technology enabled us to stay connected in different ways. Extended families could log into a virtual meeting simultaneously, churches enhanced or began offering their services online, working remotely gave people more time with their families, and businesses found new opportunities to serve customers in non-traditional ways.

Burn the Plow: A Story of Surrender

Another historical event that has changed and continues to change lives throughout generations is the death and resurrection of Jesus! As followers, we believe in the birth, death, and resurrection of Jesus Christ.

- God came to earth in the form of a human through a virgin birth. (Luke 1:34)
- Mary was a young girl engaged to Joseph who found herself with child through the Holy Spirit. (Luke 1:27, 35)
- Mary could have been publicly stoned for her pregnancy out of wedlock. (Deuteronomy 22:20-21)
- Joseph knew the baby wasn't his and was ready to divorce her until an angel appeared to him to convince him differently. (Matthew 1:19)
- Joseph and Mary wed and raised Jesus. (Matthew 1:24)
- Once Jesus began his ministries, he called twelve disciples equipped to carry on the mission after his death with the help of the Holy Spirit. The disciples were average people, not religious leaders. (Luke 6:13-16)
- People followed Jesus, listening to his teachings, experiencing his miracles, and trusting him. (Matthew 8:1-3)
- People witnessed the miracles of raising people from the dead, healing, and changing lives (Matthew 8:14-17)
- People endured persecution to follow Jesus. (John 15:18-25)
- Mary, Jesus' mother, his disciples, and all others who followed and loved him, watched his horrific death on Friday. Their hope died! (John 19:25-27)
- On Sunday, Mary Magdalene went to the tomb. When she saw it was empty, she cried. She assumed someone had stolen the body of Jesus. (John 20:1-2)

Perspective

- Jesus appeared to Mary Magdalene, and she told the disciples He was alive. (John 20:16-18)

As a Jesus follower, it must have been incredible to learn from Him, watch Him perform miracles, and experience Him healing the sick. The excitement that Jesus created as He traveled from town to town changing lives would have been incredible to witness. Then, after only three years of public ministry, His time on earth ended. Although He told His disciples that He would leave them, they didn't understand what He meant. When Jesus was arrested, tortured, and crucified, His followers experienced a wide range of emotions from fear, anger, despair, and hopelessness. As a mother, I think of the anguish and helplessness that Jesus' mother must have felt watching what was happening to her son. Friday was a dark day filled with bleakness. Little did they know, everything was about to change. When Mary Magdalene went to the tomb Sunday morning, she was filled with sadness only to find Jesus' body missing. How much more grief could one person handle? It was at that moment hope was restored as Jesus appeared to Mary! Oh, the excitement she must have felt! Hope is alive!

Sometimes we feel hopeless, just as I did during COVID, thinking about next month's revenue and trying to navigate turbulent waters. I remind myself that my view of the situation is limited to the present; I can only see Friday. God's perspective is very different from my limited view. He sees Sunday! By focusing on God and trusting in Him in times of darkness, I can be more like Job and praise God in the good and bad times. In Matthew 6:25, Jesus tells us not to worry about our lives. In Matthew 6: 32-33, He tells us the

Father knows what we need, and if we seek His kingdom and righteousness first, all these things will be added. Remember, Sunday is coming! Hope is alive! God will bless us more than we can imagine.

Life is gonna pull you down
Make it hard to see
But a little change in your point of view
Could be just what you need

There's always a reason
To always choose joy
There's something deeper
That the world can't destroy
Smile, when you think you can't
Smile, get up and dance
Smile, there's a bigger plan
The storm only lasts for a while
So smile
"Smile" performed by Sidewalk Prophets

Reflection:
1. Where is the quiet place that you can go to spend time focusing on and listening to God?
2. What are those turbulent waters you are facing? Have you reached out to God to calm them?
3. In what situations are you asking God, "Why me?"
4. Have you ever asked God to reveal what you need to learn in this situation or season? What were the results?
5. How have your friends supported you in difficult times?
6. Which areas in your life have you made decisions based on emotion instead of logic?

Perspective

7. Have you responded more like Job or his friends in difficult times?
8. Identify a significant event that happened to you that changed you. Was it a positive or a negative change?
9. What steps can you take to keep focused on Sunday in times of hopelessness?

Songs of Encouragement:
1. "Into the Sea" performed by Tasha Layton
2. "Smile" performed by Sidewalk Prophets

Chapter 6
COMPARISON

"Each one should test their actions.
Then they can take pride in themselves alone,
without comparing themselves
to someone else."

Galatians 6:4

"Keeping up with the Joneses" was a popular expression growing up. In simple terms, it is comparing what you have to your neighbor. For example, if a nearby resident bought a new car, everyone else in the neighborhood needed a new car too! In my house, we didn't keep up with the Joneses. My dad's philosophy was the opposite – if they jumped off a bridge, would you do it too? My first recollection of comparing myself to others was watching the Brady Bunch. Unbeknownst to my four-year-old self, the Brady's were not a real-life family but a TV family. I was an only child. I thought it would be fun to have siblings! Another saying I learned the meaning of very quickly was to be careful what you wish for. Two months before my fifth birthday, my wish came true. My little brother arrived, and my life as the only child and only grandchild was about to change forever!

Like many siblings, my brother and I are different in every aspect – differences that go far beyond gender. I am amazed how siblings can come from the same parents, grow up in the same house, live in the same neighborhood, go to the same schools, and be so different. In Psalm 139:13,

Burn the Plow: A Story of Surrender

David writes, "For you created my inmost being; you knit me together in my mother's womb." God doesn't create us as robots, so of course we will be unique and different! This truth is key to understanding why we shouldn't compare ourselves to others! Each of us has strengths and weaknesses. We, unfortunately, spend too much time focusing on our shortcomings and comparing ourselves to others instead of developing our God-given strengths.

Growing up, I loved attending school because I enjoyed learning, loved being around my friends, and was a good student. The night before the first day of school was like Christmas Eve for me. The anticipation of a new school year and new experiences made it difficult for me to sleep. My brother's perspective of school was much different. He struggled in school due to an undiagnosed learning disability that wasn't identified until he was in the 3rd grade.

Unfortunately, in the 1970s and 1980s, support for learning disabilities in schools was minimal, and he didn't receive the help he would have today. Since he was six grades behind me in school and we didn't have the same teachers, I don't believe he lived in my shadow. However, he may say otherwise! My brother's strengths are in the trades, not academics. Having the ability to go to a vocational school for high school saved him; otherwise, he probably would not have graduated.

Unfortunately, my parents didn't always appreciate the differences my brother and I had. We all have strengths and weaknesses, and no one should feel ashamed of their own unique traits. After graduating high school, I earned an associate degree, took two years off of work, and returned to get my bachelor's degree. Since my brother and I were

Comparison

six years apart in school, I graduated with my bachelor's degree the same year he graduated from high school. My brother barely made it through school. I, on the other hand, graduated with honors from college. My brother was not at my college graduation and was unaware I graduated with honors. All honors recipients were recognized in the printed program. The statement that my mom made as she held that program is etched in my brain forever. She said, "We don't want your brother to see this." Wait… what? I had worked hard to graduate with honors and to get scholarships. We couldn't celebrate my accomplishments because my brother might feel bad? The way my mother handled that situation was a learning moment for me on how not to treat your children! Differences should be celebrated, not hidden.

Because of our contrast, my parents treated us very differently. They were much stricter with me. When I would question the disparity, their response was because he was a boy, and I was a girl! UGH!!! As an adult, having raised two daughters, I have a different perspective on how my parents raised my brother and me. I don't believe it had anything to do with gender. Instead, my parents expected more from me because they saw my potential and wanted me to succeed. Today, I am very grateful for the way my parents raised me, and I recognize my brother is the one who has suffered.

I don't know if my parents were so focused on getting my brother through school that they ignored his behavioral issues or didn't know what to do. My brother was angry and violent; unfortunately, I was the brunt of much of his behavior. As I mentioned before, I tend to be a perfectionist, so keeping my possessions nice was essential to me. I got a babysitting job the summer after my 7th-grade year, so I could buy my own clothes and didn't have to depend on my parents. I loved the independence of having my own money that I earned.

Inevitably, my brother was always touching my things and ruining them. While this may sound like jealousy on his part, I think it was just him being spiteful! I remember finally getting a ten-speed bike. It had a gray frame with colorful pinstripes. I loved that bike and was proud of it. All my friends had a ten-speed bike, and now I had one too! One day I noticed my bike was muddy, and the pinstripe was scratched. My brother had struck again. He had taken my bike without permission and messed it up! I was furious, but my parents' response was a simple, "Don't touch your sister's things." Of course, that did nothing! This lack of justice was one of many, many examples.

The worse part was the wrath of his anger. Let me summarize by saying that it was only by God's grace that my family didn't experience the story of Cain and Abel in reverse. Cain was the oldest son of Adam and Eve, and Abel was the younger son. In chapter 4 of Genesis, we learn that Cain is working in the fields, and Abel kept the flocks. The Lord was pleased with Abel's offering but not with Cain's. Cain was angry and killed his younger brother, which sent Cain into a life of exile, although the Lord protected him from death. Unlike Cain, my brother's anger issues were much broader and not just limited to his sibling. Because my brother struggled to manage his anger, I vividly remember times where he threatened me with weapons including a shotgun. One day as I was standing in the kitchen and he was in the garage, he got mad at me about something and came at me with a sledgehammer. To protect myself, I closed the door, and he took his anger out on the door instead of me leaving a huge hole. Again, I give all the credit to God for protecting me.

To escape my brother's wrath and my parents' nonchalant attitude, I left my family's home as soon as possible, but not without so many great lessons that would help me navigate life. A few years ago, I was interviewed for a radio show, and the host asked me a question no one ever had. How did events in your childhood prepare you for your career in human resources? It was probably a question he asked everyone, but to me, it was thought-provoking. I never thought about the connection before, but as I pondered the question, I discovered that my childhood instilled in me some core beliefs. Here are a few:

1. God made us unique – we have different gifts, and we should celebrate those gifts!
2. Regardless of what happens, don't play the victim. Don't blame others for your choices.
3. Comparison leads us down the wrong roads. Keep your eyes on your own path.

Understanding our Gifts

Psalm 139:14 says, "I am fearfully and wonderfully made; your works are wonderful." David praises God's work, recognizing that He is the artisan who hand-crafted each of us. When we think or speak negatively about ourselves, we are criticizing God! When we compare ourselves to others and believe we don't measure up, we are accusing God of making us incorrectly. Instead, we should turn our doubts into an opportunity to learn about our God-given gifts and talents and focus on developing those.

In 1 Corinthians 12:8-10, Paul shares the spiritual gifts distributed by the Holy Spirit. Historically, as I read this passage, I have focused on determining my spiritual gift(s) while ignoring the verses before and after. In 1 Corinthians 12:4-6, Paul writes, "There are different kinds of gifts, but the same Spirit distributes them. There are different kinds of service, but the same Lord. There are different kinds of working, but in all of them and in everyone it is the same God at work." These gifts are distributed for the common good, not for selfish advantage. I also believe that we shouldn't compare our offerings to others but rather invest our energy in developing our gifts for the glory of God!

To make his point to the church, starting in 1 Corinthians 12:12, Paul uses a practical example that everyone can understand, the human body. The body is one unit but comprises many parts with distinct purposes; we don't expect our heart to function like kidneys. I know what some of you are thinking. Some body parts can be removed or damaged, but our bodies continue to operate. You may feel that you are an appendix, tonsils, or gall bladder and what you have to offer is not significant to the success of the "body." STOP! That is negative self-talk. God has given each of us a purpose. Although Paul is speaking to the church about the importance of each one using their gifts in the church, this is also true in our relationships, homes, schools, work environments, sports teams, etc.

Another example of many different parts working together towards one goal can be seen in an elementary

Comparison

school. There are many adults serving students, but not all in the same capacity. Is any one role the most important? Without teachers, the students could not learn. But without the principal, the faculty wouldn't have the support and leadership to enable them to teach. Without the custodians and lunchroom staff, the students wouldn't have an environment conducive to learning, and without the bus drivers to deliver them reliably and safely to school, many students wouldn't be there for teachers to teach. Even those playing the smallest roles in the students' lives have a direct impact on their education. Every single day.

In *The Maxwell Leadership Bible*, John Maxwell describes leaders as "Brokers of Gifts." Therefore, leaders are not responsible for doing all the work of the church or the organization but rather for allowing everyone to use their gifts to build great teams. Below are ten practical takeaways to consider from Paul's letter:

1. The team pursues the same goal but possesses a variety of gifts or positions.
2. Everyone has a contribution to make, which benefits the team.
3. God is the source of each gift, so He deserves the glory.
4. God chooses who has what gifts, so we must not compete or compare.
5. Team members are to function like the organs and muscles in the body.
6. No team member is less important than another; all are necessary.
7. Sometimes, the players who seem less critical are most important.

Burn the Plow: A Story of Surrender

8. God's goal is team harmony and mutual care.
9. Although members are equally important, they are meant to be diverse.
10. We should not *compete* with each other but *complete* each other.

If you are a leader at home, church, work, school, or team, have you ever thought about being a broker of gifts? It is common in organizations to focus on employee weaknesses and how to improve those shortcomings. I will often ask company leaders, what would your organization look like if you focused on developing employee strengths instead of focusing on employee weaknesses? I'm reminded of the adage, "Everybody is a genius. But if you judge a fish by its ability to climb a tree, it will live its whole life thinking it is stupid." In other words, we aren't all designed to accomplish the same tasks.

Full disclosure, I have never been to a football practice. Still, my perception is when a quarterback shows up for training, the coach will focus on developing skills such as leadership, communication, throwing and handing off the football, but NOT kicking because that's not the quarterback's job. Just as we aren't all equipped to do the same things, we aren't all called to do the same things. Just like in my school example above, the bus driver isn't called to lead the staff meeting, the principal isn't called to make the meatloaf, and the lunch lady isn't called to teach math. Therefore, we should focus on identifying and developing our strengths so we can use God's gifts in the capacity for which they were intended.

One of the attractions of the human resource profession for me is the opportunity to do in real life just what we

Comparison

have been talking about here – help people to identify their strengths, develop their power, and allow them to do what they do best. Recently, I took the CliftonStrengths® Assessment from Gallup to identify my strengths. My top strength is Individualization. When I saw this as my maximum strength, my initial thought was disappointment because I love people and teams; this had to be wrong. However, as I read through the description, my initial assumption was completely wrong – individualization didn't mean I liked to work alone. As defined by CliftonStrengths®, individualization means to be intrigued with the unique qualities of each person. Leaders with this strength excel at figuring out how different people can work together productively. Working with individuals and teams to identify their strengths and how to effectively utilize them has become a favorite part of what I do through my business.

Blaming Others

The second valuable lesson of my childhood that has helped me in my career is learning not to fall into a victim mentality. According to WebMD, victim mentality is when a person believes they have no control over what happens in their life – bad things happen to them and they blame others. They take no responsibility and problems are never their fault. Victim mentality evolves as a defense mechanism because they don't know how to cope with adverse life events. In other words, it is a learned behavior and can be changed.

As a young adult, I was unaware of what victim mentality or victimhood was. It would have been easy for me to blame the decision to leave my family home before completing

Burn the Plow: A Story of Surrender

college on my brother's behavior. I made the choice at the time because I thought it was best for my protection and own mental well-being. Looking back, I have felt I acted too hastily and should have stayed to finish college and save money to be better prepared to live independently. However, I chose to leave based on what I knew at the time as a nineteen-year-old. Several years later, I finished college, earned an MBA, and began a very successful career. Today, my experiences have helped me to trust God and to have better discernment than when I was nineteen.

Throughout my career, there have been successes and disappointments. My first full-time job was short lived. I was hired as an auditor in the company's accounting department, and in less than one year, the company filed for bankruptcy and closed. I needed to find another job quickly as I had recently moved out of my parent's house and was a newlywed. I was disappointed that I needed to find another job. God showed up and provided me another position in perfect time. Not long after I joined the new organization and began to get comfortable, they went through a restructure. Although I was able to keep my job, many of my co-workers lost theirs. It left me wondering how long it would be until my position was eliminated. The uncertainty I felt in both of these situations left me disappointed. When we experience disappointments, we have two paths we can choose.

The first path is the victim approach, claiming the outcome was unfair and blaming others. This results in feelings of jealousy and resentment. Losing my first job due to bankruptcy and then moving to another company that went through a restructure made me question why this kept happening to me. Finding a new job in the 1980s was very different than today. It required searching the Sunday newspaper, typing resumes and cover letters on typewriters, waiting on the post office to deliver my resume, and hoping to hear from the employer through a landline telephone. The process was very stressful. After sending out numerous resumes, and not receiving a phone call, it was very disappointing. It was easy to blame the employer for not considering me. I could have continued on this path, but rather I chose the other option.

The other option we can choose when faced with disappointment is to look inward and ask, "What do I need to do to get where I want to be?" When I realize I am going down the victim-mentality path, I must stop, seek God, and listen to Him. Instead of feeling envious about what others have earned or received, I focus on what I need to do to succeed. There is nothing wrong with taking inspiration from others, looking at someone's achievement and aspiring to it. It's when we are envious and covet what they have that we lose sight of our own path. A few words of advice: first, remember God created us uniquely. My success may not look like another person's success. It was at this point, I decided to return to school to complete my degree.

Second, we must ask ourselves if we are willing to do the hard work. Several years ago, I had the opportunity to hear John Maxwell speak in person. He shared that people come to him after his presentation and tell him they love what he does and want to do it too. He responds, "I know you want to do what I do, but will you do what I did?" Yes, I was willing to do the hard work; I continued to work full-time while attending school.

Burn the Plow: A Story of Surrender

We live in a world of instant gratification and expect everything now. We want our food fast, our packages delivered tomorrow, and our search engine results in a nanosecond! When we look at social media and see others' successes, we think we should have it too. However, we don't see all the behind-the-scenes hard work the person put in to get there. I hear people say they want to retire when they are 60, but they do nothing to prepare. Instead of saving and investing, they are spending money trying to keep up with the Joneses! They end up continuing to work while their friends who saved enjoy retirement. In the work environment, employees expect promotions and pay increases but fail to invest in their professional development. Then they blame others for their lack of advancement.

We see an example of blaming others in the opening chapters of the Bible. In Genesis 2, God gave Adam the beautiful Garden of Eden and charged him with taking care of it. God also told Adam he could eat from any tree except for one. God then created Adam's mate, Eve. Genesis 3 begins with the serpent questioning Eve about the tree in the middle of the garden, the only one whose fruit she'd been told not to eat. The serpent lied to Eve, tempting her to eat from it. She did. Because it was so good, she shared it with Adam. Once they realized what they had done, they tried to hide from God. When God questioned Adam, what did he do? Adam responded to God by saying, "The woman you gave me, gave me the fruit and I ate it." Adam blamed God and Eve – God for giving him Eve and Eve for giving him the fruit. The blame game continued, and Eve blamed the serpent. God didn't accept these excuses from Adam and Eve, and there were

Comparison

consequences for their decisions. It is easy to blame others for our circumstances, but if we fail to take responsibility for our own poor choices, we may continue to make them.

Going the Wrong Way

The third lesson I learned was that when we compare our situation to others or become impatient, rather than waiting on God, we make poor decisions. As I mentioned previously, I moved out of my family home at a very young age because of the environment. I was choosing my path forward based on the path I saw others take.

After high school graduation, my dad committed to pay for me to go to college. Instead of going away to a four-year college, I lived with my parents, commuted to a two-year business school, and earned a degree in accounting. After graduation, I got married and moved out. I was in such a hurry to be independent and out from under my parents' roof! Years later, I realized my dad's offer was a great deal, and I should not have been so impatient. I could have gone to a four-year college, lived on campus, and graduated debt-free! Although I eventually went back to school to complete my bachelor's and master's degrees (not subsidized by my parents), I missed out on so many experiences that many of my adult friends talk about and the lifelong friendships they made in college. This is a prime example of how I compared my path to others and tried to follow theirs instead of the path intended for me. But I remember that God has me where he wants me today is where my focus needs to be. I will not look back on my past and regret missed opportunities.

Burn the Plow: A Story of Surrender

Making life choices based on the success of others will most likely cause us to make poor decisions. Sometimes we are not content with what God has given us, and we believe we deserve something better or more. When we compare our life to others, jealousy and envy creep in, and we turn our focus to others instead of focusing on God's blessings. In James 3:14-16, we are told, "But if you harbor bitter envy and selfish ambition in your hearts, do not boast or deny the truth. This thought does not come from heaven but is earthly, unspiritual, of the devil. For where you have envy and selfish ambition, there you will find disorder and every evil practice."

As we read about King David in the Old Testament, we learn that David loved God, and God chose him to lead the people of Israel. King David was very successful, and the nation prospered. But, like us, King David did not always make the best choices, and his actions were not always pleasing to God. King David learned this very lesson when he coveted another man's wife.

The story unfolds in 2 Samuel Chapter 11. King David remained in Jerusalem while the Israelite army destroyed the Ammonites and besieged Rabbah. As he was walking on the palace rooftop, a beautiful woman named Bathsheba caught his attention as she was bathing nearby. David was intrigued by her and learned she was the wife of one of the soldiers. Once David found out who she was, he sent his messengers to get her and bring her to the palace, where he slept with her and she became pregnant.

Because the punishment for adultery was death, David devised a scheme to cover up his sin. He requested that Bathsheba's husband, Uriah, be sent home from the war so he could sleep with Bathsheba and appear to be the father. But Uriah chose not to spend the night with his wife Bathsheba because he didn't feel right enjoying himself while the others were risking their lives on the battlefield. King David had Uriah sent back to fight on the frontline so he would be killed in battle. After Bathsheba mourned her husband, she moved into the palace and became one of King David's wives. King David had multiple wives, but he still coveted another man's wife. His selfish behavior ultimately led to a path of adultery, deceit, and murder. God was displeased with David's actions, and there were consequences for his sins.

We may look at King David's story and wonder how someone could go to such extremes. We have all experienced times when jealousy, envy, and temptation crept into our minds. Once those thoughts or feelings appear, what we do next is crucial. Do we let them control us, or do we take control of them?

I make it a practice to recognize and congratulate the success of those around me by posting a congratulations on social media, sending a handwritten note, or acknowledging their accomplishment in person. When I feel those moments of jealousy creeping in, I remind myself that someone else's success does not define or detract from mine. Instead, my achievement is based on God's individualized plan for me. My key performance indicators come from God; God doesn't give us all the same key performance indicators or opportunities simultaneously.

I recently saw a saying, "Don't measure your progress with someone else's ruler!" Wow! That sums up comparison and is such a great visual for me. Next time you compare yourself to others, remember that God created each of us differently. We each have our own purpose, which is different

Burn the Plow: A Story of Surrender

than someone else's, and God moves us through our journey in different ways and varying speeds. So, let's focus on using God's ruler to measure our success. Wherever we are on our journey, let's choose joy and enjoy the place we are; we will move through our journey in God's timing.

Reflection:
1. What events in your childhood shaped who you are today?
2. As a child, what is your first recollection of comparison?
3. As a leader (at home, church, school, work, etc.), do you take on everything yourself, or do you use your energy to showcase others' strengths and give them opportunities to develop?
4. Describe a time when someone was successful and it caused you to feel jealous. What did you do?
5. Describe a time in your life when someone's success inspired you to invest in yourself so you could be successful.
6. Have you blamed others for bad choices you made?
7. Describe a time when you compared your situation to someone else's, and you made a poor decision as a result.

Songs of Encouragement:
1. "Relate" performed by FOR KING + COUNTRY
2. "Stained Glass Masquerade" performed by Casting Crowns
3. "Truth Be Told" performed by Matthew West and Carly Pearce

Chapter 7
NOT THIS OPPORTUNITY

"There is a time for everything, and a season for every activity under the heavens."

Ecclesiastes 3:1

Imagine a beautiful, sunny, summer day. You are driving a convertible with the top down along a breathtaking coastline. Ocean smells abound as the breeze blows through your hair. The fresh air on your face invigorates you as you crank up the radio and sing your favorite summer tunes. Then suddenly, everything comes to a halt. You see road signs prompting you to detour due to a road closure ahead. You now find yourself on an unfamiliar path even your GPS does not recognize. The only guidance system left is your navigation intuition. You believe you are headed in the right direction, but you soon arrive at a dead end. You turn around and try another road and end up in another dead end. You are in a maze and can't find the way out!

Our journey through life can sometimes feel like that. We experience times when we are happily speeding along on the course we have chosen. Then the path before us abruptly changes, and we experience roadblocks, detours, and dead ends. They signal to us "this is not the way" or "this opportunity is not for you." These messages can leave us with a feeling of rejection, confusion, fear, and even anger. The truth is many detours and dead ends protect us from something ahead or reroute us to something better.

Burn the Plow: A Story of Surrender

If the road ahead is unsafe, a detour provides us with a secure route. And a dead-end forces us to abandon our current direction, turn around, and look for a better way. When things don't go the way we want, perhaps we should look at it not as a disappointment, but as protection or an opportunity for something even better. It's not rejection; it's redirection.

My first memorable rejection occurred in 4th grade selling Girl Scout cookies. In the 1970s, my neighborhood was safe to sell door-to-door in the area. Most people were very generous and would buy at least one box of cookies since the price was affordable at $1.25 per box. However, there was the rare occasion when someone would say, "no, thank you." It was at that time I realized rejection is uncomfortable. However, I didn't let the rejection stop me; I simply moved on to the next house. In fact, I was usually the top seller of cookies in my troop! I l learned early in life that rejection could inspire me rather than defeat me.

Early in my career, I believed I was called to be a public-school teacher. The last semester in college was my opportunity to student teach and put into practice everything I had learned over the past few years. I had the best student teaching experience! I was paired with a teacher who was also a Christian. She was an amazing mentor. After graduating with a degree in Business Education, I was eager to land my first full-time teaching job. Unfortunately, business teachers were not in high demand. I spent the next two years substitute teaching. I was in the running for a full-time teaching position at least twice during my tenure, but I was not chosen.

Being rejected was disappointing, and after two years, I realized the public school system was not where God wanted me. I was being rerouted or detoured. This was my opportunity to change direction, and it was also when my children were born. I worked part-time in the evening at a local business school, teaching classes for working adults who wanted to earn a business degree. After a few years, I finally had an opportunity to teach full-time at another business school. All my hard work in college was paying off, not in a public school, but in a private business school.

I didn't realize it at the time, but God was preparing me for a change. Prior to my teaching career, I had worked in the business environment in accounting and human resources. I found myself teaching business courses but questioning my qualifications to do so with my limited business experience. God prompted me to return to the business world in a human resource role. Not only was God encouraging me, but He provided me with a fantastic opportunity that would change my professional direction.

One day between classes, an alumnus of the school where I had taught walked into my office. He was the CFO of a local company looking for an HR professional for their young organization. This encounter was from God! I followed up with the CFO to express my interest, and as a result, I was hired! My career was about to take off in a direction I would never have dreamed of.

Throughout my journey, I have learned there are several reasons why God might be telling me "Not this opportunity." Here are a few:

Protection – We are being protected from something. In most cases, we will never know what God detoured us from by closing a door or rerouting us. However, there are situations where God's hand is unmistakable. A few examples:

Burn the Plow: A Story of Surrender

- In December 1911, Milton and Catherine Hershey traveled to France to spend several months in Nice. Mr. Hershey planned to return to the U.S. on the ill-fated maiden voyage of the RMS Titanic in April 1912. However, due to a business situation back in Pennsylvania, Mr. Hershey needed to return to America early and left France on April 6, boarding a different ship. Catherine decided to extend her stay in Europe with traveling companions. In a postcard to Milton Hershey's mother, Catherine reflected on the sinking of the Titanic and gave God credit for their safety.
- On September 11, 2001, Cantor Fitzgerald lost 658 employees working in the World Trade Center that fateful morning, almost 2/3 of their workforce. The only reason the CEO survived was that he wasn't in the office. It was his son's first day of kindergarten, and both he and his wife took their son to school. They were in their son's classroom when they learned of the attack. There are numerous stories of individuals who were rerouted that morning in ways that kept them safe from the terrorist attacks.

God's hand of protection reminds me of being a parent of a toddler. If you have ever spent time with a toddler, you know they have no understanding of boundaries or danger, and they are fast! Parents must always keep an eye of protection on their toddlers to keep them safe. Parents are constantly saying "no" or redirecting their toddlers because they love them and want to protect them. God loves us and wants to protect us, so He will close a door or reroute us. In most cases, we will never know the danger we faced because God saved us.

Not This Opportunity

Timing – God's timing is not my timing. God thinks in terms of eternity; we think in finite terms of seconds, minutes, hours, days, weeks, years, etc. So, when we pray, and God doesn't answer our prayers after a few times, we give up. Sometimes, we may have been praying for years for healing, a spouse, a job, or in Abraham and Sarah's situation, a baby.

In Genesis 15, we read about God's covenant with Abram (Abraham's original name). God promises Abram that he will have a son and compares the stars in the sky to Abram's offspring. Abram believed God and trusted him even though his wife Sarai (Sarah's original name) was barren, and Abram and Sarai were old, well beyond childbearing age. But in Genesis 16, things take a turn; Sarai grows impatient, believing that she will never be able to have children, and forces the situation by creating a plan involving her maidservant. Sarai's goal was to have a family through her maidservant, Hagar, and Abram agreed! What just happened? In the last chapter, Abram trusts God, and a few verses later, he is sleeping with Sarai's maidservant. Abram and Sarai were desperate and saw this as the only way God's promise would be fulfilled. Going outside of God's will result in consequences. When Hagar became pregnant, Sarai despised her and the baby, which resulted in drama and a dysfunctional family at best! Hagar gave birth to a baby boy named Ishmael; Abram was 86 years old.

Although sin has consequences, God will never leave us. He loves us! His desire is for us to get closer to Him and turn from our sin, not for Him to abandon us. Abram and Sarai's story takes another turn, but not immediately. Fourteen years later, God appeared to Abram and told him to walk before Him and be blameless, and the covenant between God and Abram would be renewed. God changed Abram's name to Abraham, making him the father of many nations. God also changed Sarai's name to Sarah and promised to bless her with a son. Abraham was skeptical because he would be 100 years old, and Sarah was 90 when the baby arrived. God revealed to Abraham that the son would be called Isaac. In Genesis 21, Sarah became pregnant and bore a son. Abraham named him Isaac as directed by God.

I can relate to Sarah. I am a problem solver and can be impatient. I thrive on overcoming obstacles, crafting solutions, and executing a plan. Let's get it done; let's move forward. Followers expect leaders to make decisions and move ahead. For success, however, it is essential to slow down, yield to God for timing and direction, and *then* move forward. Being patient is something I continue to learn, to not jump ahead of God. Everything works better in God's timing! In the end, God will get us where we need to be, but we may have taken the long way to get there. If we had just waited for God and trusted Him, we could have gone His way with less pain and heartache.

Yes, I am one of those drivers when there is a backup on the highway, I will go 10 miles out of my way on back roads instead of sitting in a jam! I don't know if I gained or lost time, but I am moving! I recently saw a meme on social media with a picture of a hallway with closed doors on both sides labeled "Until God opens the next door, praise him in the hallway." In my heart, I know God is using this time in the hallway to prepare me for the next door to open, and I should use that hallway time to seek God's direction. To be honest, I will start out seeking God's guidance, but as time

Not This Opportunity

passes, I begin to get impatient, and it won't be long until I knock on those doors or turn the knobs.

The lyrics from John Waller's song "While I'm Waiting" speak to how we should respond to our hallway time:

> While I'm waiting, I will serve you
> While I'm waiting, I will worship you
> While I'm waiting, I will not faint
> I'll be running the race even while I wait

God has something better for us – Remember Jeremiah 29:11 tells us that God has plans for us, plans to prosper us, and not harm us, plans to give us a hope and a future. How do we know if this is the right timing? Perhaps Abram and Sarai believed Hagar was God's plan for them. John Maxwell shares practical guidelines from King Solomon in Ecclesiastes 3:1-8 when it comes to timing. We don't control the timing of events. The best we can do is recognize and respect God's plan.

1. It is our responsibility to recognize God's timing.
2. It is our responsibility to accept and cooperate with God's timing.
3. Our alignment with God's timing makes a significant difference.
4. God has made everything appropriate in its time.
5. God has put eternity in our hearts, so we must trust God to communicate His timing.
6. We can do nothing better during our lifetime than to rejoice and do good.

God wants us to trust Him and grow our faith. Therefore, He will not reveal His plans ahead of time. I can trust God in uncertain times because I can look back on the many times He provided for me in the past.

Moving from a full-time employee to a self-employed independent contractor resulted in giving up a guaranteed biweekly paycheck and paid time off. Therefore, when I submit a proposal to an organization for a project and I hear no response, or they select someone else, I have learned to trust that another opportunity exists. God has continually shown up and provided for me so often that when that proposal does not translate into a revenue opportunity, I am learning that my emotion should no longer be disappointment but rather excitement to see what else God has in store for me! That bears repeating – not getting what you want can actually be a reason for excitement, rather than disappointment, as you see what God has planned for you!

Learning to say no. I desire to help people succeed, and it is hard for me to say no because I don't want to disappoint or turn someone away. Unfortunately, this desire resulted in seasons where I was overwhelmed and overextended. John Maxwell often tells us to say no to the good so we can say yes to the best. This is a lesson I am continually learning, but I am making progress.

Several years ago, the ladies' Bible study at my church spent several weeks unpacking the book of Esther using Beth Moore's material. As we were in this book, I fell in love with the lessons of Esther, and it really impacted my understanding of God's timing. The entire book of Esther is about God's providence. The notes I wrote in my Bible include:

Not This Opportunity

1. God is setting things up.
2. God is working behind the scenes.
3. Providence can only be seen in hindsight.
4. We must live in faith now.

If you have never read the book of Esther, I encourage you to take some time to do so. It will probably take you the same amount of time it would to stream one episode of your favorite show. The book of Esther, however, is much more suspenseful, and you will walk away with great lessons!

The backstory of the book of Esther is King Xerxes of Persia was having a royal party. Apparently, they spent a lot of time partying in those days. After several days of drinking and celebrating, the King called for Queen Vashti to come and display her royal beauty to the men attending the party. Queen Vashti did the unthinkable and refused. The queen was expected to go to the king when he requested and only at his request. Disrespecting the king came with harsh consequences, and Vashti was banned from ever seeing the king again. The search was on for a new queen throughout the land, and Mordecai, a Jew, took his niece Esther to the citadel of Susa, where women were being introduced to the king. Esther never revealed her nationality and won favor with everyone, including the king. She became the next queen. I know, it sounds like the story of Cinderella!

While Mordecai was sitting at the gate, he overheard two of the king's officers plotting to assassinate the king. Mordecai shared this information with Esther, who reported it to the king, ensuring Mordecai was given credit. The king's men were hanged, and a man named Haman was elevated to the king's highest seat of the nobles. Mordecai refused to

Burn the Plow: A Story of Surrender

bow to Haman, who became enraged. Once Haman learned that Mordecai was a Jew, Haman wasn't satisfied with killing just Mordecai; he wanted all the Jews destroyed. Haman convinced the king that the Jews needed to be destroyed, so a decree was issued.

Mordecai went crazy! A maid told Esther about Mordecai's behavior, and she sent someone to find out what was happening. Mordecai pleaded with Esther to go to the king to beg for mercy and plead for her people. Remember, the king was not aware that Esther herself was a Jew. Also, no one could approach the king without being summoned; otherwise, the consequence was death. The only exception was if the king extended his gold scepter to the person approaching him, he would save their life.

Esther was conflicted at this point. If she approached the king, she could be killed, but if she did nothing, she and her people would perish. This is where the most famous quote from this book is found. In Esther 4:14, Mordecai was convincing Esther that she needed to go to the king and he said to her "…. that you have come to a royal position for such a time as this."

At this moment Esther reflected on all God has done for her, and she realized her unique opportunity to protect the Jews. God gave her the wisdom to develop a plan and the patience to carry it out, which included fasting and prayer. Esther approached the king about holding a banquet for him and Haman; remember, the king loved a good party! What happens in the remaining chapters is a fantastic story of a reversal of destiny – yes, the good guys win! However, there are some great lessons to be learned from Esther.

Not This Opportunity

1. Esther had to overcome her fear. As King Xerxes' wife, God had put her there for a reason, and she was chosen. But because there was no guarantee that the king would spare her life if she approached him without permission. She had no choice but to trust God.
2. Esther played it cool. She and her people were facing death, and the gallows were being built. Yet, she took time to pray and fast and wait for God. She was patient even in a time of urgency.
3. God is always working; we may not see it. We just need to wait on His timing so He can prepare for us.

The overarching theme for me is to not get ahead of God. If Esther had approached the king before God had all the pieces in place, the results could have resulted in death for Esther and the Jews. The king asked her on two occasions about her request, but she waited to share until the timing was right. Because of the situation's urgency (the Jews were about to be killed), I am not so sure I would have been as patient as Esther. But Esther trusted that God was working in the background.

So, when she shared her request, the king's eyes were opened and he was willing to grant all she asked. Sometimes, an idea pops into my head that excites me, and I know I need to take time to pray and listen to God before I move ahead. Over the past few years, I have had to put this into practice. Now that I am responsible for securing my income, evaluating revenue opportunities while using my time wisely and efficiently is critical to ensure I focus where God wants me, and I don't get distracted and drift off course.

Burn the Plow: A Story of Surrender

Staying the course has been a challenge for me due to two factors. First, I believe God has called me to come alongside people on their journey to be successful, and I want to say yes to everyone! Second, I have always been independent when it comes to earning money, and I want to make sure I can pay the bills. Therefore, meeting my revenue goals is essential. All the opportunities may be good, but are they the best? Learning to discern when to say yes and when to say "not this opportunity" is a journey I am currently traveling.

Recently, I read the book *The Vision Driven Leader* and listened to a podcast by its author Michael Hyatt about the importance of a written vision script. These two resources have benefited me as I work to stay focused on my vision and not get distracted, causing a mission drift.

1. A written vision statement or script is a 3-to-5-year direction of where I am going and what is essential. This vision becomes my filter between what is a significant opportunity and what is a distraction that masquerades as an opportunity. As more opportunities present themselves, I get overwhelmed. My vision script helps me discern what is a vision-aligned opportunity and what is an opportunity that distracts me from the vision.
2. My mission describes my situation now. It is my purpose – what I do and why I do it.
3. My strategy is how I get from my current situation to my vision. This can change frequently based on current events.
4. My values are who I am and who I am becoming.

Not This Opportunity

This process was beneficial as I was writing this book. My vision – or maybe God's vision for me – for many years was to write a book. I finally got serious about it when I wrote down the vision. Once I had the written vision, I began putting a strategy together – how do I get from ten bullet points to a published book? My strategy included both working with a book coach who could guide me through the process and being intentional about setting time aside each week to spend writing. I blocked out Wednesday mornings on my calendar weekly so nothing else would be scheduled. I stood firm and said "no" to many opportunities (distractions) that would have filled up those Wednesday mornings.

There were limited occasions that I had something important that interfered with my Wednesday mornings, but I always made sure to find another day in the week when I could spend a few hours writing. Having this focus was freeing to me. This may sound strange, but I found freedom in saying "no" to an opportunity because I could justify my response. It is not always easy to say, "not this opportunity," but it has been worth it in the end. God continues to bless me beyond my expectations.

In Ecclesiastes, we can learn from King Solomon. He was wise, experienced many things, and accumulated wealth, none of which fulfilled him. He concluded that life is meaningless. If we remove God from the equation and fail to understand our vision and purpose, we will chase after things that do not bring us joy and fulfillment. In *The Maxwell Leadership Bible* in Ecclesiastes 2-11, John Maxwell identified practical questions to ask as we determine where to invest our time and energy. I have found these questions extremely helpful as I decide if each opportunity is aligned with my vision or a distraction.

1. Is this opportunity consistent with my priorities?
2. Is this opportunity within my competence? Maybe I need to invest in learning.
3. Can someone else do it better, or does it align with someone else's vision more than mine?
4. What do my trusted friends say?
5. Do I have the time?

As my journey continues, remembering to change the "no" into "not this opportunity" is a challenge for me. The proper perspective is recognizing that "no" is not a negative but rather God protecting me from something or preparing me for a better opportunity that fits with His vision. During this hallway time, when I am waiting for the next door to open, I will focus on preparing for the better opportunity He will provide. While I am in the hallway, there will be distractions posing as opportunities, and I must be able to discern the difference so that I have the capacity when God opens that next door for me.

Reflection:
1. When was your first experience with rejection? Did you give up or move on?
2. When did you experience rejection but later experience a better opportunity than you could have imagined?
3. Have you ever had a "hallway time?" If so, describe what you did in the hallway.
4. Describe a time when you were growing impatient waiting for God and took matters into your own hands.

5. Do you have a written vision? What would a written vision look like for you?
6. What is your strategy to achieve your vision?
7. What are three things you need to do to move from where you are to where you want to be?
8. Where in your life do you need to start saying "not this opportunity" so you can stay focused on your vision?

Songs of Encouragement:
1. "While I Wait" performed by Lincoln Brewster
2. "While I'm Waiting" performed by John Waller

Chapter 8
RELATIONSHIPS

*"Greater love has no one than this,
that he lay down his life for his friends."*
John 15:13

For most of us, our first understanding of relationship is our family. As a five-year-old, I have many memories of my mom, dad, and myself. As an only grandchild, I spent significant time with my paternal grandparents. Unfortunately, my grandfather died suddenly when I was three, but I have fond memories that I have been able to hold on to for many decades. I am also fortunate to have had the opportunity to grow up with cousins. Unlike my dad, who was an only child, my mom has four siblings, which meant fun times with cousins. As a child, I remember spending weekends at my maternal grandparents' home with my aunts, uncles, and cousins, celebrating holidays, harvesting and freezing corn, or visiting. In the summer, my grandfather would break out the ice cream maker, and we would take turns churning to ultimately share in the reward of homemade ice cream. Although my family wasn't perfect, I feel blessed that many positive memories far outweigh any bad ones.

As I think about the importance of relationships, the one word that keeps coming into my mind is investment. As I reflect on the relationships in my life, the person I see as someone who has spent her life investing in others is my mom. As a child, she poured into me more than just making

Burn the Plow: A Story of Surrender

sure I was clothed, fed, and had a safe place. She supported me in all my activities, whether financially, with time, or with other resources. She volunteered in my Girl Scout troops, went on field trips, and attended all my softball games and chorus concerts. When I was in elementary school, she would pack my lunches. Although we didn't have 'Lunchables' (prepackaged kid meals) in the 1970s, she would cook noodles for me and put them in a thermos container right beside my sandwich, packing it in my lunchbox every morning.

As I mentioned, my mom supported me in my Girl Scout activities and held many volunteer leadership positions, eventually working for the Girl Scouts full-time in their office. Her first position was Registrar. She was responsible for making sure the scouts and leaders were registered for a local troop. In the spring and summer, she registered the girls for summer camp. However, I believe her favorite position was being the Administrative Assistant to the property manager and the camp rangers. During her 25 years working for the Girl Scouts, she invested time to ensure girls had the opportunity to experience a positive camping experience and that the property manager and camp rangers had the tools and resources they needed to be successful in their positions.

My mom has a passion for serving others. When I was a teenager, we joined a church where many of my friends were in the youth group. My mom immediately became active on the kitchen committee. She spent almost 40 years serving in that role, shopping for food, preparing, serving, and cleaning up. It seemed like she was at church all the time, or at least that was the message I would hear from my dad. She invested in the people and families in the church. Whenever

Relationships

there was a need for food at church – whether it was Lenten dinners, funerals, coffee breaks, celebrations, meetings, youth fundraisers, Fasnacht day, etc. – she was there!

As my grandparents were aging, my mom would spend as much time as possible caring for them. My paternal grandmother and my mom didn't have the closest relationship, and this was not my mom's fault. Keep in mind I don't have sons; however, I believe there is a unique relationship between mothers and sons. I always suspected that regardless of who my dad married, she would never have been good enough for my grandmother! My grandmother didn't drive, and when my dad wasn't available, my mom would make sure my grandmother got to the grocery store, her hair appointments, doctor appointments, and other places she needed to go. When my grandmother started having health problems, my mom stepped up and was there to support her, regardless of how my grandmother had treated her in the past. I believe my grandmother appreciated my mom over the years but may not have said it.

While my mom was caring for my paternal grandmother, her parents, who lived more than an hour away, were also aging and needed support. So, my mom would leave work, drive to my grandparents' house to spend the night, and drive back to work the following day. She would do this several times per week. A home health aide would come in a few nights, but my grandparents always felt more comfortable when my mom was there.

After my grandparents passed away, my mom continued to work for a few more years, eventually retiring and finding part-time jobs or volunteer opportunities. My mom loved to be busy and productive. She would step up to help anyone she could. But finally, she had to give up her volunteer opportunities and part-time jobs due to my dad's failing health.

Those who knew my parents would tell you their relationship seemed unbalanced. My mom always invested more in my dad than he invested in her. When my dad became sick, she was always by his side, sitting all day in the hospital with him. She put her life on hold to stay home with him because she didn't feel confident that he should be left alone. Again, some people would say he didn't deserve everything she did for him. My mom demonstrated the love of Jesus! Relationships are about investing in and loving people, not about whether they deserve it or not or what they can do for you. Jesus tells us in John 15:12, "My command is this: Love each other as I have loved you."

Ruth & Naomi

Investing in relationships often requires us to make sacrifices. When we make the investment and sacrifice for the right reasons, God will bless us! We can see this in Ruth's story in the Old Testament. Ruth was a Moabite woman who was married to one of Naomi's sons. Naomi's family moved to Moab because of a famine in Bethlehem. Naomi's husband and sons died while in Moab, leaving Naomi a widow with two widowed daughters-in-law.

After the famine, Naomi decided to return home, and her Moab daughters-in-law wanted to go with her. Naomi told them to return to their mother's homes and hoped they would find husbands. But they protested and wanted to stay with Naomi because they loved their mother-in-law.

Relationships

Naomi pleaded with them to return to their homes so they would have a chance at a better life. Naomi's one daughter-in-law finally agreed to return to her home. But Ruth was committed to Naomi, and no matter how Naomi pleaded, Ruth wanted to return to Naomi's homeland.

Ruth was willing to make the sacrifice to leave her country, her comfort zone, and move to a foreign land. Ruth desperately wanted Naomi's people to be her people. Finally, Naomi gave in and stopped urging Ruth to return to her home. As they arrived in Bethlehem, Ruth would go into the fields and find food for her and Naomi. Her work there ultimately led to Ruth being blessed with a husband, Boaz. Her sacrifice and commitment to her mother-in-law opened doors for her. Ruth is the great-grandmother of King David, and in Matthew 1, we see Ruth listed in the lineage of Jesus.

Ruth exemplifies how her loyalty, integrity, and commitment to doing the right thing resulted in God blessing her. In *The Maxwell Leadership Bible*, John Maxwell says Ruth illustrates that we receive blessings when we place responsibilities before results, character before conduct, and faithfulness before fruitfulness. Too often, we focus on getting the results and how we can benefit with limited investment; we want an immediate tangible return. If we don't see a quick benefit, we move on. Unfortunately, this tends to be the rule rather than the exception in business relationships, especially in sales situations. I have experienced three basic types of business relationships.

The first relationship is based on convenience or reward. As long as there is something to gain from the relationship, it will continue. However, once there is no longer a benefit derived from the relationship, it ends. The second relationship focuses on investing in each other and caring about one another, and there is no expectation about deriving a benefit or reward. All other connections are probably the third type, somewhere in between the first two. We view these relationships more as acquaintances and stay in touch in ways that are mutually convenient.

I desire to have relationships built on investing in each other. I seek transformational relationships where I can walk alongside people as they journey through life. In my opinion, having a relationship with someone to gain something of benefit is not a relationship but rather a transaction. Of course, there may be times when we need to have transactions and acquaintances, but transformational relationships – such as with Jesus, our family, friends, and other believers – are critical to our life journey because they can be a source of encouragement, accountability, and strength.

Many years ago, as I was working as the Director of HR for a small business, a salesperson from an employee benefits brokerage firm visited me to discuss voluntary employee benefits. At the time, our organization had an employee benefits broker who was good friends with the owner. The business was locked in, and there was no chance for this salesperson to get the benefits business. Most salespeople are transactional; if there is no opportunity, they will never be heard from again. But this salesperson was not like others. He continued to stop by and visit me every year. It was an opportunity to stay connected. After several years, his investment paid off for his company and me. I changed organizations, and the new organization was not committed to an employee benefits broker. Within three weeks of joining the organization, I called him, and his company earned all the employee benefits business from my new organization. The story doesn't end there. A few years later, I joined the employee benefits firm as an employee, and the salesperson and I became co-workers! Transformational relationships require an investment in others.

A Relationship with Jesus

The most powerful transformational relationship in my life is my relationship with Jesus. My relationship with Christ began as a teenager, and as I got older, my relationship grew and became more profound. Because God loves all of us, He sent his Son to save us. For most of us, John 3:16 was the first Bible verse we learned: "For God so loved the world that he gave his one and only Son, that whoever believes in him shall not perish but have eternal life." It doesn't matter who we are, what we have done, or where we are from. God sent His Son to die for all of us!

God's desire is for all of us to live in heaven for eternity and not be condemned to death. Paul tells us in Romans 6:23, "For the wages of sin is death, but the gift of God is eternal life in Christ Jesus our Lord." God does not force a relationship with us. He gives us a choice. I chose to have a relationship with Jesus so I can be secure in my future and because I know I am not alone as I go through my journey on earth. You do not have to be alone either. God may not remove the storms of life, but He won't let you go through them alone!

When you have doubts that you are not worthy of a relationship with Jesus, stop and think about Jesus' ministry as recounted in the Gospels. When Jesus walked the earth,

Burn the Plow: A Story of Surrender

His focus was not just on the religious leaders or the Jews. He focused on everyone, both Jews and Gentiles, including those who were the least respected in the community. Jesus called twelve ordinary men to be his disciples. They were not religious leaders and were in occupations unrelated to the mission to which they were about to be called.

The four men who appear to be in Jesus' inner circle – Peter, Andrew, James, and John – were two sets of brothers who were fishermen; they knew about fishing. Jesus called them from fishing boats and told them he would make them fishers of men instead of fish! Simon was a political activist, and Matthew was a tax collector and a loner. Judas Iscariot was a traitor! A relationship with Jesus is transformational, not transactional; Jesus invested in others regardless of their characteristics, backgrounds, or skill sets. As followers of Jesus, the disciples witnessed Jesus performing unbelievable miracles such as casting out demons, healing people with leprosy and other diseases, and raising Lazarus and a little girl from the dead. Jesus connected with sinners, tax collectors, and societal outcasts. No matter what you have done or how low you believe you are, Jesus does not see you the same way. He will always be there for you!

Jesus' disciples were ordinary men who were unprepared to take on the mission He had planned. However, Jesus invested in them, and, as John MacArthur said in his book *Twelve Ordinary Men*, "the legacy of New Testament Scripture and the testimony they left are still changing the world today." Jesus demonstrated servant leadership with His disciples. Servant leadership focuses on serving and investing in people. It is transformational, whereas

Relationships

traditional leadership focuses on improving the organization in the marketplace and is transactional.

Servant leaders shift the priority from the organization to the people; it isn't about the position but rather about attitude. When leaders demonstrate how people are valued and essential, people become more invested in the organization, and the organizational results may far exceed expectations. Jesus could have invited more qualified people to be His disciples, such as those with a spiritual backgrounds, strong faith, and commitment. Instead, Jesus called men who required a significant investment, but He was willing to pour into them and equip them for the ministry.

One of the best examples of servant leadership is described in John 13. The time was right before Jesus' death. Jesus and the disciples were enjoying a meal before the Passover Feast. Jesus had such a great love for these men that after dinner, He got up from the table, took off His outer clothing, wrapped a towel around His waist, poured water into a basin, and began to wash the disciples' feet and dry them. This was a task that was done by servants and was very humbling. Jesus was demonstrating an example for His disciples that they, too, should humble themselves for others.

Several years ago, I attended a corporate meeting in Orlando, Florida. Pat Williams, a basketball Hall-of-Famer, co-founder of the NBA's Orlando Magic and former general manager of the Philadelphia 76ers was our guest speaker at dinner. I was very fortunate to be seated at his table during the buffet dinner. As the attendees finished their entrees, I noticed that Mr. Williams got up and went to the dessert table and began serving dessert to the other attendees. Mr. Williams, our guest of honor, was serving others. I did

Burn the Plow: A Story of Surrender

not know much about Mr. Williams and his story, but I did notice he was demonstrating a serving heart. When Mr. Williams shared with our group, he talked about servant leadership and listed seven practical insights to be a servant leader: vision, communication, people skills, character, competence, boldness, and a serving heart.

In *The Maxwell Leadership Bible*, John Maxwell provides practical applications for investing in a servant leadership relationship with others, and I have added examples.

- **We should put others ahead of our agenda** – In a me-first world, this is counterintuitive to our culture, and it can be unpopular for us to put others first. But, as leaders, we should take responsibility for the team. As Jesus did, we should invest in the growth and development of our team members.
- **Develop the confidence and security to take risks** – For many of us, we avoid risks because we fear rejection or ridicule. Although Peter pushed back on Jesus washing his feet, Jesus stood firm and explained to Peter why this was important. With consistency in our servant leadership commitment, we can be confident when we step out of our comfort zone to serve others.
- **Look for a need and take the initiative** – If we keep our heads down and are not looking around, we miss seeing the needs of others and the opportunity to serve them. Connecting with others by being with them, observing their behavior, and talking with them will help us identify their needs and step up to address them.
- **Perform small acts anonymously** – There are hundreds of small things we can do daily to show others we see them and recognize them. For example, our tone when we communicate with each other, holding the door as we

Relationships

enter or exit a building, smiling and saying have a good day to those we pass, and sending an encouraging message are just a few small acts we can perform daily. Servant leaders are motivated to act without drawing attention to themselves. Instead, they give credit to those who deserve it, pave the way for others, and work behind the scenes to ensure others have the resources they need to be successful.

- **Learn to walk slowly through the crowd** – Everyone is in a hurry! Let's slow down and pay attention to others. How often do we ask someone how they are doing but don't take the time to listen to their response and ask follow-up questions. As the saying goes, stop and smell the roses. We tend to be thinking about the next thing and may miss what is happening right before us. We miss the opportunities to take the initiative to serve others when we move too fast.
- **Begin your day reflecting on your love for others in your life** – Jesus showed us that everyone is valuable! Too many times, we focus on people's shortcomings, not their strengths. Jesus tells us in Mark 10:45, "For even the Son of Man did not come to be served, but to serve, and to give his life as a ransom for many."
- **Develop a bias for action** – This is an opportunity for us to step outside of our comfort zones and move away from the traditional leadership approach and move toward being transformational leaders. We must start somewhere, and sometime; today is the day!

Many business cultures focus on organizational success, or the success of the leader, but not always the success of their people. Therefore, investing in others in a me-first culture can be unpopular and challenging. Servant leaders recognize that putting others first and engaging in transformational relationships are the keys to attracting and retaining top talent, which ultimately results in successful organizations. In his book *Becoming Better Together,* Dr. John Van Epp reminds us that when our primary goal of the relationship is to give, we gain, but when the primary goal is to get, we lose.

Judas Iscariot, one of Jesus' disciples, is an example of someone who used his relationship with Jesus to get something but ended up losing. The chief priests and elders were planning to arrest Jesus. Judas went to the chief priests and elders and asked what they would give him to turn over Jesus. Judas received 30 pieces of silver for turning over Jesus in an act of betrayal. When Jesus was arrested and condemned, Judas was overcome with guilt and remorse, which led him to return the money to the chief priests and elders and then take his own life.

Unfortunately, betrayals happen in relationships, both professional and personal. Perhaps you have been a victim of a betrayal or have been the one to betray someone in a relationship. When a betrayal happens, it erodes trust not only in the person who betrayed us but makes us afraid to trust others. Building trust takes time, but it can be lost in a moment. When we have been betrayed or find ourselves in an unhealthy professional or personal relationship, we have a choice in how to respond. Our first reaction is to give into our human instincts and respond based on our feelings rather than reacting the way God would have us respond. Below is an outline of how we can respond in a manner pleasing to God.

1. **Pray about the right direction.** If the betrayal occurred in your workplace, is this something that can be worked

Relationships

through, or is the environment too toxic and you need to find a new workplace? If the betrayal is in a personal relationship, is this a relationship that can be repaired, or is it unhealthy and needs to be ended? Seek God's direction! Philippians 4:6-7 says, "Do not be anxious about anything, but in everything, by prayer and petition, with thanksgiving, present your request to God. And the peace of God, which transcends all understanding, will guard your hearts and your minds in Christ Jesus." Proverbs 3:5-6 tell us, "Trust in the Lord with all your heart and lean not on your own understanding; in all your ways acknowledge him, and he will make your paths straight."

2. **Forgive others; forgive ourselves.** Paul tells us in Colossians 3:13, "Bear with each other and forgive whatever grievances you may have against one another. Forgive as the Lord forgave you." In Matthew 6:14, Jesus instructs us to pray. We should forgive others when they sin against us, and our Heavenly Father will forgive us. But, depending on the betrayal and the number of times it has happened, can we really forgive? Our human instinct is to say no because the person is undeserving. During a sermon several years ago on this topic, I jotted down a few notes in my Bible that helped me better understand forgiveness. When we forgive others, we are not releasing them from consequences. It is not the same as reconciliation, it is not a once-and-done decision, and it is not condoning the wrong. Forgiveness is a journey; when we forgive, we can move forward and not be held hostage any longer!

3. **Do not take revenge; let God take care of it.** When someone hurts us, our first instinct is to return the hurt.

This is how Satan takes a foothold! In James 4:7 we read, "Submit yourselves, then, to God. Resist the devil and he will flee from you." When Satan is in my head, I immediately go to this verse and say, "not today, Satan!" If I am alone, I will say it aloud! It is not my responsibility to bring justice to the other person. God will take care of it. Romans 12:19 reads, "Do not take revenge, my friends, but leave room for God's wrath, for it is written: 'It is mine to avenge; I will repay,' says the Lord." Instead of revenge, God tells us to feed our enemies when they are hungry and, when thirsty, give them drink; this will heap burning coals on their heads (Romans 12:20). That verse is so comforting to me! God has my back. Let go, let God!

4. **Treat others the way you want to be treated.** Jesus tells us in Matthew 7:12, "So in everything, do to others what you would have them do to you." In Romans 12:19, God tells us to treat our enemies with respect, and in verse 21, He tells us not to be overcome by evil but overcome evil with good. Revenge is about repaying evil for evil; revenge is of Satan! I don't want to be betrayed, so why would I cross the one who betrayed me? In healthy relationships, we treat others with respect. Jesus knew that Judas would betray him, but He continued to show him kindness. WOW. Jesus will never betray you!

Relationships are like gardens, and they require our time, effort, and commitment. If you have ever planted a garden, you know gardens require a lot of attention. We prepare the soil, plant the seeds, remove the weeds, water the plants, and protect the garden from harmful outsiders. Hopefully, all the hard work will pay off at the end of

Relationships

the season with a bountiful harvest. If we only threw seeds on a mound of dirt and came back months later, we would have nothing to harvest because we didn't make the appropriate investment.

As my earthly journey continues, I want to have beautiful gardens with bountiful harvests. I desire to have more transformational relationships, be a servant leader in a me-first world, and demonstrate the love of Jesus to others. Throughout our day, we can find ways to demonstrate the love of Jesus through servant leadership by investing in others – in the celebration of their successes such as a marriage, the birth/adoption of a child, graduating from college or an advanced degree program, or obtaining professional licensing or certification. Those around us also go through difficult times – such as when their loved one dies, they experience health issues, or they are facing a family crisis – and a servant leader supports and encourages them through these struggles.

Reflection:
1. What is the first relationship that you can recall? What did you learn from that relationship?
2. As you evaluate your relationships, how would you classify them? Are they transactional, transformational, or acquaintances?
3. How would you describe your relationship with Jesus? What is holding you back if you don't have a relationship with Him?
4. Do you know someone who demonstrates servant leadership? How have they shown servant leadership toward you?

5. Have you demonstrated servant leadership towards others? In what ways can you improve in the area of servant leadership?
6. Who do you need to forgive? What steps can you take today to move in the right direction?
7. Which relationships do you need to invest in? Which relationships do you need to divest?

Songs of Encouragement:
1. "You've Always Been" performed by Unspoken
2. "Forgiven" performed by Crowder
3. "Forgiveness" performed by Matthew West

Chapter 9
BUILD UP ONE ANOTHER

"Therefore, encourage one another and build each other up, just as in fact you are doing."
1 Thessalonians 5:11

I was invited to speak at an event two years before starting my own business full-time. The group organizer who asked me to speak chose to pair me with another speaker I had never met. This was new to me. Typically, I am invited to speak solo, or if I am speaking with someone, it is someone I know. I will admit I was anxious about this arrangement. Would the two of us be able to connect so that we could deliver an exciting presentation, or would the production be very clunky and disjointed? The event was a few months in the future, so there would be time for us to collaborate and get acquainted. The organizer introduced us via e-mail, and we scheduled a time to communicate over the phone. Before our phone call, I spent a little time researching the other speaker and her company. My quick search didn't result in anything substantial. I had no real background information about her.

The time came for our call, and as we introduced ourselves, I quickly realized she knew much more about me than I knew about her. She had researched me on social media and reviewed my company website; she had an advantage over me. As we spoke, it became clear that our business models, client bases, and target audiences differed.

Burn the Plow: A Story of Surrender

She shared with me that she had owned her own business for almost two decades and was very successful. I am always interested in hearing others' stories, so I was excited to learn about her unusual business name, how she started her company, and the consulting services she offered to her clients. As I shared my story with her, I explained that going full-time into my own business was new for me, and I was always open to learning from others. Perhaps I could learn from her experiences as well.

I shared with her some of the exciting things I had on the horizon and how I was looking forward to these new experiences. Unfortunately, the conversation took a strange twist at that point, and I was blindsided. To this day, I wonder if what happened next was intentional on her part, perhaps she was unaware of the impact of her words and she just thought she was being helpful. When I told her I was preparing to transition full-time in my business and I could learn from her experiences, it was as if I gave her license to criticize everything I was doing.

For the next 15 minutes (which seemed much longer), she turned everything I was excited about into negatives and reasons why I should not do those things. She had known me for just a few minutes, and instead of asking questions to learn more about my plans and intentions, she provided negative feedback! Fortunately, we transitioned into discussing the event, the topic, and the next steps. She offered to take the first step by putting an outline together. I was happy to comply because I was sure anything I provided would not be met with her approval.

After the call ended, I sat at my desk in shock! What just happened? In that short phone call, she negatively rocked my

Build Up One Another

world, and I began to doubt myself. When a situation like this happens, we tend to go into fight or flight mode. This speaking engagement was not a big event nor a once-in-a-lifetime opportunity. Therefore, my first reaction was to call the organizer and cancel.

Reacting emotionally is never a good idea, so I took a few minutes to get my thoughts together. God showed up while I sat at my desk and spoke two things. First, canceling the engagement was not an option. I should move forward and use this as an opportunity to learn. Second, and most importantly, I never want to make anyone feel the way I felt when the call ended. Maybe her coaching approach was tearing others down to build them back up, but that was not my approach, and it never will be.

This story took another unexpected twist two weeks later when God showed up again. The other speaker called me and told me she was backing out of the engagement, and I would be on my own. I never learned why she cancelled, but honestly, it was a relief! A few months later, I spoke at the event solo, and all went well. Although the original phone call was difficult, the experience resulted in a great lesson I have never forgotten. Let's build each other up! Ephesians 4:29: "Do not let any unwholesome talk come out of your mouths, but only what is helpful for building others up according to their needs, that it may benefit those who listen."

Unfortunately, there is too much tearing down of each other instead of building up one another in our society. We see it everywhere: workplaces, homes, churches, social media, television, music, sports events, and other public places. This behavior is not from God but rather from Satan. Ephesians 6:12 says, "For our struggle is not against flesh

Burn the Plow: A Story of Surrender

and blood, but against the rulers, against authorities, against the powers of this dark world and against the spiritual forces of evil in the heavenly realms."

Instead of tearing each other down with criticism and negativity, God calls us to love each other. In John 13:34, Jesus preached, "Love one another. As I have loved you, so you must love one another. By this all men will know that you are my disciples, if you love one another." A quote I have heard frequently from John Maxwell is that people don't care how much you know until they know how much you care. To positively impact others, we need to build them up, not tear them down. I can't change the world as one person, but I can start where I am, one person at a time.

Many years ago, I heard Barbara Glanz share the story of Johnny the Bagger and the one small thing Johnny did daily that significantly impacted one community. Johnny attended a convention sponsored by his employer, a large grocery store chain. Barbara spoke about creating memories for the customers so they would want to return. She gave out her phone number and e-mail address so the attendees could share great service stories.

A month after the convention, Johnny contacted Barbara and shared an idea. Johnny, who had Downs Syndrome, was a bagger at the grocery store and wanted to think of a way to make a difference. He liked sayings, and with his dad's help, they would print out a positive phrase or quote each day. Then, he would sign his name, drop the quote in each customer's bag and say, "I hope you enjoy my quote of the day."

He asked Barbara what she thought about the idea, and she told him it was fantastic! A month later, she received a call from the store manager. He shared with Barbara that one day he noticed that one check-out line was three times longer than the others, so he encouraged the customers to move to another line to shorten their wait. The customers declined because they wanted Johnny's quote of the day! One customer told the store manager she used to come into the store once a week, but now she stopped in two or three times a week just to get Johnny's quote of the day.

The store manager held a team meeting and shared Johnny's initiative to give customers more than they expected. That afternoon the store manager noticed the employee in the floral department cutting off the stems of the broken flowers and pinning the flowers on elderly women in the store. The employee in the meat department loved Snoopy and was putting Snoopy stickers on the packages and engaging in conversations with the customers. The enthusiasm was contagious throughout the store, and all employees sought creative ways to serve the customers. The employees were having fun, and the customers were happy – all because one person chose to do something different! This incredible story reminds us that no matter our position in the organization, we just need to start where we are by encouraging one person at a time. Our small acts of encouragement can be contagious!

Sometimes we feel our history stands in the way of encouraging others. When we feel embarrassment, shame, or guilt about our past, Satan is tearing us down and keeping us down. These feelings are not of God! In fact, God uses our stories, no matter how messy they are, to encourage others! In our church, one of my favorite times is baptism. Baptism is an opportunity for Christ-followers to publicly share their expression of faith in Christ to show that they are all in as His follower.

Several rows of seats are removed from the auditorium every three months and replaced with a large inflatable pool filled with warm water. Before the baptism, participants prerecord their stories, and the story is played as they walk to the pool. Sometimes, they will invite friends or family members who encouraged them in their faith journey to join them in the water as they are baptized. Once the individual emerges from the water, we hoot, holler, and clap!

It is an unbelievable experience and an encouragement to hear stories of lives changed by Christ! We listen to stories ranging from elementary-age children to adults in their 90s. Their experiences all vary – from trusting God to deal with bullies in school to individuals who spent time in prison, overcame addictions, wronged others, lived a life apart from Christ, and found how knowing Christ has changed their lives. Regardless of their messy stories, they are making them public as a testimony to Jesus. When others hear our stories, they can be encouraged that no matter what they have done or where they are on their journey, there is always hope!

The Bible is filled with many stories of encouragement that we can relate to today. However, two significant events from the New Testament are the most encouraging to me. First, Jesus called twelve ordinary men to be His disciples. He spent three years nurturing, teaching, training, and equipping them. His disciples deeply loved Him. During his three years of ministry on earth, the number of individuals who loved and followed Jesus grew exponentially. Jesus was equipping his disciples to continue his ministry because His time on earth was short, and He had a plan!

Build Up One Another

Before his arrest, Jesus shared his plan with his disciples. Understandably, they were confused about what He was saying. Jesus knew that He would have to die, and because His ministry needed to continue, His death wouldn't be the end. In John 14, Jesus told his disciples that God would send a replacement, the Holy Spirit. Depending on the Bible translation, terms used to describe the Holy Spirit include counselor, friend, helper, strengthener, standby, comforter, advocate, and intercessor. These terms have a common theme – they are terms of encouragement.

When a loved one dies, we feel a void in our lives. Sometimes we say we have a hole in our hearts; we miss them terribly! Understanding the loss in death, Jesus told his disciples that he would not leave them to fend for themselves. They would not be orphans. In John 16, Jesus acknowledged that his disciples were filled with grief but encouraged them by saying, "It is for your good that I am going away. Unless I go away, the counselor will not come to you; but if I go, I will send him to you." Jesus was telling his disciples the Holy Spirit would pick up where He left off and do more! He encouraged His disciples not to be afraid but to have peace.

Being a Christ follower doesn't mean I won't experience trouble and heartache, but through the Holy Spirit, I can have joy because I won't have to go through those tough times alone. One of the most encouraging verses to me is John 16:33 where Jesus tells his disciples that they will have trouble, but He has overcome the world! Jesus is telling us the end of the story; as believers, we can have hope!

Have you ever watched a very suspenseful movie more than once? The first time you watched it, you had no idea what would happen, so you were on the edge of your seat.

Burn the Plow: A Story of Surrender

However, the second time you watched the movie, you knew how the film ends. You felt less anxious about each plot twist because you knew what was to come. Remember, we see how the story ends whenever we experience trouble and challenging times. Jesus has overcome the world, giving us hope!

Be encouraged knowing that as a Christ believer, the same power that raised Jesus from the dead lives in us! We have a counselor, friend, helper, strengthener, standby, comforter, advocate, and intercessor available to us 24 hours each day, 7 days per week, and every day of each year! In addition, we are very blessed to have the Holy Scriptures inspired by God that we can read for encouragement. Many people have given their lives to ensure that the Bible can be accessible to everyone who wants one and translated into their language. The Bible is overflowing with encouragement in both the Old and New Testaments. A few more verses that bring me motivation under challenging times include:

Joshua 1:9	"Be strong and courageous. Do not be terrified; do not be discouraged, for the Lord your God will be with you wherever you go."
Psalm 46:10	"Be still and know that I am God."
Proverbs 3: 5-6	"Trust in the Lord with all your heart and lean not on your own understanding; in all your ways acknowledge him, and he will make your paths straight."
Lamentations 3: 22:23	"Because of the Lord's great love we are not consumed, for his

	compassions never fail. They are new every morning; great is your faithfulness."
Jeremiah 29:11	"For I know the plans I have for you, plans to prosper you and not to harm you, plans to give you hope and a future."
Romans 8:31	"If God is for us, who can be against us."
Philippians 4:6-7	"Do not be anxious about anything, but in everything, by prayer and petition, with thanksgiving, present your requests to God. And the peace of God, which transcends all understanding, will guard your hearts and your minds in Christ Jesus."
Philippians 4:13	"I can do all things through him who gives me strength."
1Peter 5:6-7	"Humble yourselves, therefore, under God's mighty hand, that he may lift you up in due time. Cast all your anxiety on him, because he cares for you."

These are some of the many verses that encourage me daily. When I am going through challenging times, I know it is just a season, and it is in these times that I need to lean into God through the Scriptures, prayer, and songs. I listen to Christian music on my drive home when I have a tough day at work.

Burn the Plow: A Story of Surrender

A few years ago, my father got sick and spent months in the hospital and rehabilitation hospital. Once he was released from the rehabilitation hospital, he was not able to come home, so he was transferred to a nursing home. We thought he would be there for a short time and then be able to return home. He was there less than a week when my mother received a call in the middle of the night. Only a few hours after she left him, he was found unresponsive and taken to the hospital and put-on life support.

My husband and I had a trip to New York planned for that weekend. My mom encouraged us to go on our trip while the doctors diagnosed my father. We were attending a Chris Tomlin concert at Madison Square Garden when I received a message from my mother telling me that my father was brain dead. In the middle of singing praise to Jesus, I learned my father would never return to us. During that time, I continued to sing to Jesus for comfort because I knew the days ahead would be difficult.

The next day we returned home to visit with my father and my family. We knew that we would have to make the decision to remove him from life support. We decided as a family to gather at the hospital the next day to meet with his doctors. My father had a living will and we knew of his wishes. The doctors told us that once the life support was removed, it could take hours or days for him to pass. Adding to my struggle was the fact that our daughter's birthday was in two days. I did not want him to pass on her birthday.

My mother, brother, and I made the decision to remove the life support. We gathered in my father's room and my husband led us in prayer before the nurses came in. Six hours after the life support was removed, he passed. Having to make the decision to remove the life support was the most emotional decision I have ever been through. But I could feel the love of Jesus surrounding and comforting me. Prayer, Scriptures, and Christian music helped me through the grieving process.

The second significant event in the New Testament that I find encouragement from is the story of Saul/Paul. Earlier, I shared how Saul, who persecuted and killed Christians, had a radical transformation with God. This encounter not only led him to become a Christ-follower but an apostle and one of the most influential leaders in the Christian church. Some of Paul's letters of encouragement to Christ-followers are found in the New Testament, which continue to be an encouragement to us today. As I read through his letters and learned about his life after his transformation, these characteristics are what I love about Paul and are an encouragement to me.

1. **Focus** – In Philippians 3:13-14 Paul tells us to keep the goal as our focus. He writes, "Brothers, I do not consider myself yet to take hold of it. But one thing I do: Forgetting what is behind and straining toward what is ahead, I press on toward the goal to win the prize for which God has called heaven-ward in Christ Jesus." Paul did not have an easy journey toward the goal. Even after he and Silas were flogged and imprisoned, Paul had a single-minded passion. As they sat in prison, they prayed and sang hymns to God. Because of Paul's and Silas' focus on God, the jailer and his household believed and were baptized. Our journeys will not be easy either; they are filled with detours and distractions, but if we

keep our focus on the goal God has given us, we will get there. Every day we are faced with distractions that pull us away from our goal. Sometimes distractions are Satan reminding us of our past or others demanding our attention and resources. As I continue my journey, I am working to improve my discernment around which opportunities help me move toward my goal and which are merely a distraction.

2. **Humility** – Paul remained humble throughout his ministry. In Timothy 1:15, Paul refers to himself as the worst sinner, but God's grace is more significant than all of Paul's sins. In 2 Corinthians 12:7, Paul refers to a thorn in his flesh to keep him humble and from becoming conceited. Although Paul pleaded with God to remove the thorn, the thorn remained. Instead, God revealed to him that His grace is sufficient, and His power is made perfect in our weakness. We need the thorn to keep us dependent on God and humble. Paul knew exactly who he was and was very open about his past; he demonstrated vulnerability. Because Paul named his shame, shared his guilt, and gave God the glory, people could connect with him. This reminds us to be authentic and keep our eyes focused on God. Our past sin does not hinder success if we remain humble and let God's power be made perfect in our weakness. I have confidence that God's grace is more sufficient than all my sins!

3. **Cheerful Greetings** – When I receive notes of encouragement, I keep them to read in difficult times when I need positive words. We are fortunate to have some of the many letters Paul wrote during his ministry to encourage us. Paul always begins his letters with

encouragement and reminds his readers of the love of Jesus. When Paul received news that the church in Corinth was experiencing problems such as division, immorality, idolatry, false teachings, and pride – many of the same issues we have today – he wrote letters to the people. Paul's letters were to confront them about sin, speak the truth in love, and encourage them. In his letter to the Galatians, Paul needed to bring the Galatians back on course. They were drifting away from the Gospel and even perverting it. He needed to remind them what Christ did for us. Paul's letter was to motivate, correct, and encourage. One specific verse that can inspire us back on track is Galatians 5:1 "It is for freedom that Christ has set us free. Stand firm, then, and do not let yourselves be burdened again by the yoke of slavery." When we find ourselves drifting, we need someone to get us back on the right course before it is too late! Paul recognized the danger of drift and desperately wanted to get the Galatian church to acknowledge the departure and course correct.

4. **Hope** – Paul continued his ministry even in the midst of difficult circumstances. Paul was beaten and imprisoned but continued to send letters of encouragement and hope. While in prison, Paul wrote letters to believers in Ephesus (book of Ephesians), Philippi (book of Philippians), and Colosse (Colossians). Paul continued to focus on the mission and not his circumstances. Paul kept his eyes focused on Jesus, and it paid off. Paul knew the enemy was defeated, and while in prison, Paul wrote encouraging words in Colossians 2:13-15 that we are alive in God. He has forgiven our sins, canceled

the law, disarmed the authorities, and triumphed over them. He has defeated the enemy! We have hope because we know how the story ends; our troubles are temporary!
5. **Mentor** – Great leaders recognize the potential in others and mentor them. Mentoring is walking on the journey with those with less knowledge, experience, and skills and encouraging them to develop and grow in their potential. As we see in the Scriptures, both Jesus and Paul were leaders who invested in teaching and equipping others, ensuring the ministry could continue and grow long after they were gone. Paul mentored many people, most notably Timothy. Paul planted a church in Thessalonica, but was abruptly forced out. However, Paul did not give up; he continued to mentor and encourage the new leaders in the Thessalonian church via letters. Paul's life was in danger if he had returned to Thessalonica. So, he sent his protégé, Timothy, who could confidently minister to the people of Thessalonica as Paul would have and report back to him on their progress. Some leaders are hesitant to mentor others for various reasons, most likely because of insecurity – they fear the mentee will outperform them. For other leaders, we are honored and humbled to be asked to mentor others.

As I read through Paul's letters, I am encouraged by his passion, humility, focus, and love toward Christ and others. The same power that raised Jesus from the dead and the same power that transformed Saul into Paul is living in me. The best part is knowing that the Holy Spirit wasn't limited to the disciples – as a Christ follower, I too have the Holy

Spirit living in me! I know I will go through difficult times and struggles, but I won't go through them alone!

Reflection:
1. In your workplace, church, or community, identify small acts of encouragement you can show others.
2. What obstacles are standing in your way to being an encourager to others?
3. Who do you need to encourage? In what ways can you encourage them?
4. Who has encouraged you in the past?
5. Which verses in the Bible bring you comfort?
6. Describe a time when you went through a storm, and God's word encouraged you.
7. What is your compass or GPS that keeps you focused?
8. What is the "thorn" that God has not removed from you to keep you humble?
9. Have you had a mentor relationship with someone? Were you the mentor or mentee? How did this relationship impact your life?

Songs of Encouragement:
1. "See a Victory" performed by Elevation Worship
2. "Goodness of God" performed by Bethel Music
3. "Resurrection Power" performed by Chris Tomlin

Chapter 10
OPEN MIND, OPEN HEART, OPEN HANDS

"Humble yourself before the Lord, and he will lift you up."
James 4:10

The year before I wrote this book, I had the opportunity to meet a human resource professional who started her consulting business about the same time I began mine. We knew each other's name, had many colleagues in common, and worked for the same client, but we had never met. I was planning a seminar in her area, and I felt God nudge me to reach out to her and find out if she was interested in partnering with me. Although our business focus differed, some of our services crossed over.

This collaboration could be intimidating to some people because they would view us as competitors, and why would anyone want to partner with their competitor? I am not scared about this type of partnership, but I was curious how she would respond; would she welcome a collaboration or reject it. I have plenty of experience knowing that when God nudges, following His leading results in a positive outcome. So, I took a chance and reached out to her. We had an enjoyable conversation getting to know each other, and we discovered quickly we had so much in common. As we discussed our approach to business and competition, we had the same philosophy – that of abundance, not scarcity.

Burn the Plow: A Story of Surrender

As my friend and colleague shared her story with me, it became apparent why God nudged me to reach out to her. Her story aligned with my vision for this chapter, and I asked her if I could share her story. Below is Angela's story in her words:

Differentiate. Find your niche. Be the most arrogant person in the room. I've received a lot of this type of advice as an entrepreneur and solo human resources and talent development consultant since opening my practice in 2019. I started to follow that advice – all of it – and found myself personally conflicted.

You see, all the advice and thoughts about being a small business owner were provided by amazingly talented experts and those who run successful businesses. Most of the advice was shared with good intentions, and I was open to receiving it. However, once I started applying it, mainly when I found myself in conversations with others comparing what I do to individuals claiming to be in a similar space, I ended up frustrated. I was spending my time and mental energy selling myself – trying to explain my services to others or what makes me unique, listing my qualifications and credentials, and overall working hard at building a business and finding more clients. Mentioning a competitor's name left me stressed and overwhelmed.

Then, something happened, almost overnight, quietly whispering to me all along, perhaps a prompt from God or divine intervention. I had had enough differentiating, specializing, competing, and explaining, and I opened my hands and heart. That's right, I decided when I found myself in conflict with myself or others, trying to apply the advice or questioning it, I opened my hands–literally and figuratively. I realized there are many pieces to an infinite pie, and we do not have to compete.

Yes, I made an untested and unscientific decision you will not find in any guru's course, business book, or best practice publication–ever! I opened my hands to receive work, serve others, and be open to opportunities and partnerships. Almost overnight, I received requests for services and proposals for projects, most unsolicited and none expected. Coincidental? Perhaps, yet I believe it is more providential, and I am not turning back.

This shift in thinking and the simple act of physically and mentally opening my hands, heart, and business to opportunities has been a blessing. It has led me to new partnerships and projects because I have been willing to explore, engage, and connect. I lead with my heart and head, and I cannot wait to see where my open hands commitment takes me and my business next. Opening my hands has been my best business decision ever.

Abundance vs. Scarcity

Angela describes an abundance mindset when she refers to the many pieces of the infinite pie. Understanding the differences between an abundance and a scarcity mindset and learning to live in a place of abundance can be life changing. It begins with perspective. As humans, we are wired with a scarcity mindset. We are taught that resources are limited from a young age. When I was a child, certain foods were limited, and my parents did not allow me to eat

Burn the Plow: A Story of Surrender

as much chocolate as I wanted in one sitting. Once the candy was gone, there was no more. As I grew older, I learned that money was limited. I was told that money does not grow on trees – it is a limited resource. We transfer those lessons we learned as a child and apply them to our adult situations and get stuck in that scarcity mindset.

From an economic perspective, we are taught the concept of scarce resources. The demand for the resource is greater than the supply of the resource, and therefore, the cost is driven up. The most notable resource many of us feel a scarcity around is money. I promise not to go too far into the economic weeds for fear of losing you! Money is limited only when we demonstrate a scarcity mindset regarding our opportunity to earn more. Our ability to increase our income is relatively high. Businesses identify additional market opportunities to expand market share, non-profit organizations evaluate opportunities to find new revenue sources and donors, and individuals develop their skill sets to improve their prospects for better-paying positions. However, if we look at all opportunities through a scarcity mindset, we will remain stuck in our current situation without hope of moving forward. Changing our mindset from scarcity to abundance requires us to change our perspective.

To begin the shift, we must understand the difference between abundance and scarcity mindsets.

Abundance Mindset	Scarcity Mindset
Possibilities and Opportunities	Limitations and limited resources
Grateful	Fearful and full of anxiety

Open Mind, Open Heart, Open Hands

Generous & share with others	Holds on to everything/hoards
Proactive	Reactive
Think big, audacious goals	Small goals, stay in comfort zone
Competes to better themselves	Competes against others
Encourages others to be successful	Resents others' success
Optimistic	Negative thoughts/victim mentality
Craves growth	Knows everything, limited growth

In a "Minute with Maxwell" episode, John Maxwell describes the difference between abundance and scarcity, like an ocean vs. a reservoir. The ocean waves are never-ending, whereas a reservoir can dry up. Changing our perspective from scarcity to abundance is a choice. How we view things is how we do things. Scarcity mentality is all around us, so how do we change our perspective to one of abundance?

In his book *The Seven Habits of Highly Effective People*, Steven Covey refers to the abundance mentality as believing that there is plenty out there for everyone. Alternatively, someone with a scarcity mentality believes there is only one pie out there, and if someone gets a big piece of the pie, it means less for everyone else. Covey believes one way to develop an abundance mindset is to associate and spend more time with people and mentors who have an abundance mindset. Being around people with an abundance mindset allows one to see it in practice. Otherwise, if we constantly associate with people who have a scarcity mindset, there is no opportunity to witness a different perspective play out.

In an article from July 2020, *Forbes* identifies the following five ways to move from a scarcity to an abundance mindset. I have identified Scripture to support each one.

1. **Focus on what you have and find the good.** It is believed that Paul wrote the letter to the Philippians while in prison. Despite his circumstances, Paul continued to encourage others and focus on the good. In Philippians 4:8, Paul's wrote, "Finally brothers, whatever is true, whatever is noble, whatever is right, whatever is pure, whatever is lovely, whatever is admirable, if anything is excellent or praiseworthy, think about such things." Each day let's commit to finding the good in every situation and being grateful for what we have.
2. **Surround yourself with people who have an abundance mindset.** Proverbs 27:17 says, "As iron sharpens iron, so one man sharpens another." One piece of iron by itself will be dull and useless. But, for both blades to become sharp, they need to sharpen each other. When we connect with others with an abundance mindset, the same happens to us. We are sharpened and improved by our interactions with them.
3. **Create win-win situations instead of one person winning and another losing.** During my career, I have witnessed employees in the same organization compete against one another instead of working together for the good of the organization and customers. In addition to breeding distrust and resentment among colleagues, this can result in a loss of efficiency, productivity, customers, and employees.

Open Mind, Open Heart, Open Hands

As a leader, it benefits your team to find ways to make a win for one be a victory for all. I am grateful that God promotes a winning mindset! God has prepared a place for all of us in eternity with plenty of space for everyone. In John 14:2, Jesus tells us, "In my Father's house there are many rooms, I am going there to prepare a place for you." In perhaps the most well-known verse in the Bible, John 3:16, Jesus says, "For God so loved the world that whosoever believes in him shall not perish but have eternal life." We can all go to heaven if we believe we are sinners and Jesus died for our sins. We don't have to compete with each other to get into heaven. Everyone is welcome!

4. **Incorporate gratitude into your life.** We have seasons in our life when everything is going well, and we feel full of gratitude, and then there are those times of trouble when we can barely make it through the day, much less feel grateful. In Paul's letter to the Thessalonian church, his final instructions tell them to always be joyful, pray, and give thanks in all circumstances (1 Thessalonians 5:16-17). James has a fascinating perspective on trials and tribulations. In James 1:2-4, he begins his letter by stating that we should consider it pure joy when we face trials. You read that correctly, and it grabs the reader's attention! James continues by explaining that when we face trials, our faith is being tested, which develops perseverance so we can be mature and complete, not lacking anything. I have a note in my Bible that says, "no shortcuts." This process is necessary for us to grow and mature! Paul shares the same perspective in Romans 5:3 where he writes, "We also rejoice in our sufferings because we know suffering produces perseverance,

character, and hope." As both James and Paul wrote these words, they knew hope would not disappoint. God will be by our side during our trials and tribulations through the Holy Spirit. We just need to keep our eyes focused on the hope of God, not the struggle.

5. **Train your mind to recognize the possibilities.** As we read through the Scriptures, we are continually reminded of situations that seem impossible from a human perspective. Still, as written in Luke 1:37, nothing is impossible with God. Zechariah and Elizabeth were childless even though they observed God's commandments and regulations. One day an angel appeared to Zechariah in the temple and shared that he and Elizabeth would have a son. Zechariah and Elizabeth were older; therefore, Zechariah didn't believe the angel, and he was silenced until his son was born. During Elizabeth's pregnancy, an angel appeared to Mary (Elizabeth's cousin), who was young and engaged to Joseph, and shared that she had found favor with God and would give birth to a son, Jesus. Mary was a virgin and did not understand how this could happen. According to science/human perspectives, these two women should never have been pregnant, but God! Paul reminds us in Philippians 4:13, "I can do everything through him who gives me strength." The Scriptures also tell us that Jesus raised from the dead a widow's son (Luke 7:11-15), a young girl (Luke 8:50-56), and Lazarus (John 11:38-44). Again, nothing is impossible with God!

With the above list, *Forbes* has provided great suggestions on how to move towards an abundance mentality. However, this list is not all-inclusive. For me, the best way to move from fears of scarcity to an abundance mindset is to focus on God through prayer, Scripture, or song. When I feel the scarcity mindset creeping in, it is a warning sign that I must spend more time focusing on God. The Scriptures are full of examples demonstrating God's provision when there seemed to be lack of something, and by spending time reading those examples, I can be assured He will continue to provide.

Ephesians 3:20 is an example of God's abundance mindset where Paul writes, "Now to him who is able to do immeasurably more than all we ask or imagine, according to his power that is at work within us." This is quite a promise. Not only is God able to meet our needs, but He is able to do immeasurably more! That's the very idea of abundance – more than enough. People with an abundance mindset are open to sharing with others because they trust that there will be more than enough, whereas those with a scarcity mindset will hoard everything for fear of running out.

Generosity

Merriam-Webster identifies the following synonyms for generosity: abundance, openhandedness, unselfishness, philanthropy, and open-heartedness. These are very positive words that most of us would be proud to have used to describe us. We don't have to be wealthy to be generous. Generosity is about giving! Giving of time, money, resources, kindness, love, etc. Sure, rich people can give more money than someone on a fixed income, but generosity is about attitude and sacrifice.

In Mark 12:41-44, we read about how Jesus was watching people put their money into the temple treasury. Wealthy people gave large amounts, while a widow put in two small

Burn the Plow: A Story of Surrender

copper coins worth a few cents. Jesus told the disciples that the poor widow put more in than all the others because they gave a small portion of their wealth, but she gave everything she had. The widow gave a small amount, but it was a sacrifice. You may have the same question: If the widow gave all her money, how did she buy food and necessities? Jesus doesn't tell us how that story ended, but through other verses, we can be assured she was well cared for.

- **Matthew 6:33** – "But seek first his kingdom and his righteousness, and all these things will be given to you as well."
- **2 Corinthians 9:6-8** "Whoever sows sparingly will reap sparingly, and whoever sows generously will also reap generously. Each of you should give what you have decided in your heart to give, not reluctantly or under compulsion, for God loves a cheerful giver. And God can bless you abundantly, so that in all things always, having all you one, you will abound in every good work."

Mark 6:30-44 tells a story I learned as a child, the story of Jesus feeding the five thousand. Jesus and the disciples needed rest. Jesus recommended they go to a quiet place to get some rest. However, the crowds followed Jesus to a remote location so they could learn from him, and the sick could be healed. Jesus had compassion on them and began teaching. It was getting late, and since it was a remote place, there was no food to feed the crowds. The disciples were concerned and asked Jesus to turn the masses away so they could go to the villages to get food. Jesus told the disciples to feed the crowds. I typically have an abundance mindset, but in this situation, the scarcity mindset would have been front and center! The disciples pushed back, saying it would cost eight months of wages to feed the crowd. Jesus directed them to find food in the group; he didn't want them to buy it. The disciples went into the crowd and were able to find five loaves and two fishes, surely not enough to feed the public. They demonstrated a scarcity mindset. Jesus directed the disciples to have the people sit in groups. Jesus took the five loaves and two fishes, looking toward heaven, gave thanks, and broke the loaves. He gave them to the disciples and directed them to divide the fish. Everyone had plenty to eat, and twelve basketfuls remained.

Here are a few lessons from this miracle:

1. This story is told in all four gospels – Matthew, Mark, Luke, and John – and the accounts by the four authors are very similar.
2. Jesus demonstrated compassion. He was tired, but he didn't turn the people away. He was generous with his time.
3. Jesus delegated tasks in order to bless others. The disciples were directed to find food and feed the crowd. (Their involvement allowed them to understand first-hand how little food there was to feed the crowd and what a miracle it was that it was sufficient. By experiencing the need and then witnessing Jesus fulfill that need, they were just as blessed as the people who were fed!)
4. Openness is demonstrated by the boy who gave the food (John 6:9). The boy could have easily refused to sacrifice his meal and instead made sure his own needs were met. A note I jotted in my Bible many years ago says, "God never asks us to give what we don't have, but He can't use what we will not provide." The boy was open to

giving Jesus his lunch, and Jesus could do more with it than anyone could imagine.
5. Jesus is demonstrating that it isn't about how much we have – it is about how open we are to giving it to God to bless and multiply it. Jesus took food intended for one and used it to feed 5,000 people (with leftovers).

We should focus on finding ways to be generous with the resources God has entrusted to us. Generosity isn't limited to money – we can give freely of our time, talents, and kindness. Those small acts of kindness can go a long way to brighten someone's day and will encourage you too! Transitioning from a scarcity mindset to an abundance mindset will open possibilities we could never imagine. It will take patience, time, and commitment to be abundance focused. Trust in God, and He will do immeasurably more than we can imagine.

Friends, we have come to the end of the book, but my journey does not end here, and it is not the end of your trip. I am anxiously waiting for God to show me the next steps in my journey. We are each on a unique and personal expedition and at different places along our journey. I pray this book will inspire you along your path, wherever you may be. You may be stuck and need help figuring out how to start again. Or you may be going down the wrong road and need to turn around. Or you may be on a detour or at a crossroad and unsure which direction to go. Don't let fear, failure, shame, guilt, and worry (all distractions from Satan) stop you from moving forward. Regardless of your current situation, count on God as your guiding light.

Proverbs 3:5-6: "Trust in the Lord with all your heart and lean not on your own understanding; in all your ways acknowledge him, and he will make your paths straight."

Open Mind, Open Heart, Open Hands

Isaiah 30:21: "Whether you turn to the right or to the left, your ears will hear a voice behind you, saying "This is the way, walk in it."

Philippians 3:14: As a Christian, Paul describes our journey. "I press on toward the goal to win the prize for which God has called me heavenward in Christ Jesus."

At the end of my earthly journey, when I arrive in heaven, I hope to hear the words Jesus spoke in the parable of the talents, "Well done, good and faithful servant!" **Matthew 25:23.**

Final Thoughts

Listening to Christian music is one of my favorite ways to worship God! Therefore, it seems fitting to give final thoughts based on lyrics from a particular song. Not long after I started writing this book, I heard a song that shook me to my core called *Make Room* by Meredith Andrews. As I listened to the music, with tears rolling down my face, an overwhelming prompting came over me that this song would close out my book. As you read these words, I pray that you are filled with the Holy Spirit and surrender to God's way.

> Here is where I lay it down
> Every burden, every crown
> This is my surrender
> Every lie and every doubt
>
> And I will make room for you
> To do whatever you want to do

Burn the Plow: A Story of Surrender

Shake up the ground of my tradition
Breakdown the walls of all my religion
Your way is better
Come do whatever you want to
You are all I'm chasing now

When we surrender to God and Burn the Plow, He will never leave us. He will accompany us on our journey in good and bad times. When we open our heart, hands, and mind, God will do amazing things. It is time to burn the plow! Let go, Let God! May God bless you!

Reflection:
1. Identify ten good things in your life right now.
2. Did you grow up in an environment that promoted an abundance or scarcity mindset?
3. Which areas in your life do you need to move from a scarcity mindset to an abundance mindset?
4. How can you be more generous?
5. What area of your life are you holding on to and need to open your hands and heart to God?
6. Where are you on your journey? What do you need to help you move forward?

Songs of Encouragement:
1. "Make Room" performed by Meredith Andrews
2. "Same God" performed by Elevation Worship
3. "I Surrender" performed by Hillsong Worship

ENDNOTES

Chapter 1

Furtick, Steven: Greater: Dream Bigger. Start Smaller. Ignite God's Vision for Your Life. 2012; published by Multnomah Books, Colorado Springs, CO

Chapter 2

Furtick, Steven: Unqualified. 2016; published by Multnomah Books, Colorado, Springs, CO

Chapter 3

Kilner, John, F.: Dignity and Destiny: Humanity in the Image of God. 2015; published by Wm. B. Eerdmans Publishing Co, Grand Rapids, Michigan

Matthews, Kenneth: The New American Commentary. 1996 B&H Publishing Group, Nashville, TN

Shirer, Priscilla: The Armor of God. 2015, 2018 Lifeway Press, Nashville, TN

Chapter 4

Lencioni, Patrick: Five Dysfunctions of a Team. 2002 Published by Jossey-Bass, San Francisco, CA

Chapter 5

Maxwell, John: Maxwell Leadership Bible. 2002, 2007, 2014, 2018. Thomas Nelson Publishing, Nashville, TN

Burn the Plow: A Story of Surrender

Chapter 6

Maxwell, John: Maxwell Leadership Bible

Chapter 7

Maxwell, John: Maxwell Leadership Bible

Hyatt, Michael: The Vision Driven Leader. 2020 Published by Baker Books, Grand Rapids, MI

Chapter 8

Maxwell, John: Maxwell Leadership Bible

MacArthur, John: Twelve Ordinary Men: How the Master Shaped His Disciples for Greatness and What He Wants to Do with You. 2002. Published by Thomas Nelson, Nashville, TN

Van Epp, John Dr.: Becoming Better Together 2017, 2019 published by Trinity

Chapter 10

Maxwell, John: Minute with Maxwell, February 27, 2020. https://www.youtube.com/watch?v=UanEpGb429w

Covey, Steven: The Seven Habits of Highly Effective People. 1989, 2004. Free Press a division of Simon & Shuster, Inc. New York, Ny

5 Ways To Go From A Scarcity To Abundance Mindset. Forbes July 2020 https://www.forbes.com/sites/carolinecastrillon/2020/07/12/5-ways-to-go-from-a-scarcity-to-abundance-mindset/?sh=1f3915081197

SONGS OF ENCOURAGEMENT

Chapter 1

"Thrive" performed by Casting Crowns

"Burn the Ships" performed by FOR KING + COUNTRY

Chapter 2

"Firm Foundation" performed by Cody Carnes

"God of the Promise" performed by Elevation Worship

Chapter 3

"Who You Say I Am" performed by Hillsong Worship

"Image of God" performed by We Are Messengers

"Build A Boat" performed by Colton Dixon

Chapter 4

"Evidence" performed by Josh Baldwin

"Fear is a Liar" performed by Zach Williams

Chapter 5

"Into the Sea" performed by Tasha Layton

"Smile" performed by Sidewalk Prophets

Burn the Plow: A Story of Surrender

Chapter 6

"Relate" performed by FOR KING + COUNTRY

"Stained Glass Masquerade" performed by Casting Crowns

"Truth Be Told" performed by Matthew West and Carly Pearce

Chapter 7

"While I Wait" performed by Lincoln Brewster

"While I'm Waiting" performed by John Waller

Chapter 8

"You've Always Been" performed by Unspoken

"Forgiven" performed by Crowder

"Forgiveness" performed by Matthew West

Chapter 9

"See a Victory" performed by Elevation Worship

"Goodness of God" performed by Bethel Music

"Resurrection Power" performed by Chris Tomlin

Chapter 10

"Make Room" performed by Meredith Andrews

"Same God" performed by Elevation Worship

"I Surrender" performed by Hillsong Worship

ABOUT THE AUTHOR

A wife, mother, gram, daughter, and friend, Kim Nash is dedicated to the people in her life and focuses on traveling a Christ-centered journey. As a human resource professional and teacher, she has spent more than three decades training and developing others through coaching, teaching, and speaking opportunities. Kim is passionate about helping others succeed in their life journey.

Growing up in a small family business and learning the importance of a strong work ethic from her parents, Kim has dedicated her life to being a role model and leader for her family, friends, and colleagues. She has an Associate Degree in Accounting from Central Penn Business School, a Bachelor of Science Degree in Secondary Education/Business from York College of PA, and an MBA in Human Resource Management from the University of Phoenix.

Additionally, Kim has the SHRM-SCP certification from the Society of Human Resource Management, the SPHR certification from HRCI and has completed the John C. Maxwell Certification Program to teach, coach, train, and speak. Kim has had the opportunity to speak at various organizations, associations, and businesses locally and nationally.

After years of living in a comfort zone of working for others and surrendering to God, Kim stepped out in faith and started her business as a consultant. She works with a variety of organizations and leaders. Before and during her career transition, God showed up in amazing ways to give her confidence that this was the right path for her. God is now using her story to encourage others on their journey through this book.

Kim and her husband Greg live in Hummelstown, PA, and are the parents of four grown children and four grandchildren. When they are not working or spending time with their family, they enjoy the beach, and at least once per year, you can find them on a cruise ship. They attend LCBC Church in Manheim, PA, where Kim serves on the KidMin team and participates in SHE Studies, a ladies' bible study.

You can connect with Kim to share your story or invite her to speak at your event at kim@uthriv2.com. Her website is https://uthriv2.com/.

Made in the USA
Middletown, DE
05 May 2023